CHIEF

E. ROBERT JORDAN

BJU PRESS

GREENVILLE, SOUTH CAROLINA

Library of Congress Cataloging-in-Publication Data

Jordan, E. Robert, 1925-
Chief / E. Robert Jordan.
p. cm.
ISBN 1-59166-372-5 (perfect bound pbk. : alk. paper)
1. Jordan, E. Robert, 1925- 2. Baptists—Clergy—Pennsylvania—
Biography. 3. Baptists--Doctrines. I. Title.

BX6495.J66A3 2004
286'.1'092—dc22

2004021703

Cover image courtesy of the author

Note: The fact that materials produced by other publishers may be referred to in this volume does not constitute an endorsement by BJU Press of the content or theological position of materials produced by such publishers. The position of BJU Press, and of Bob Jones University, is well known. Any references and ancillary materials are listed as an aid to the reader and in an attempt to maintain the accepted academic standards of the publishing industry.

All Scripture is quoted from the Authorized King James Version unless otherwise noted.
Scripture quotation taken from the Amplified® Bible, Copyright © 1954, 1958, 1962, 1964, 1965, 1987 by the Lockman Foundation. Used by permission.

Chief

Cover design by Craig Oesterling
Composition by Melissa Matos

© 2004 by BJU Press
Greenville, South Carolina 29614

ISBN 1-59166-372-5

15   14   13   12   11   10   9   8   7   6   5   4   3   2

It would appear that if you write a book you are expected to dedicate it to someone. With me that does not present a problem. Most pastors in full-time service have met and fellowshiped with precious saints of the Lord. Out of the multitude that I have met, I chose just one to whom to dedicate this book.

I dedicate this book to my dear wife, Marjorie Brooks Jordan. In my opinion she is the greatest believer I have ever met. She is a great soulwinner and pastor's wife, also my secretary for the past sixteen years.

CONTENTS

Preface   **vii**

Acknowledgments   **viii**

Introduction   **ix**

The Battle for My Soul—Salvation   **1**

My Battle as a New Believer   **16**

The Battle to Get into Full-Time Service   **22**

The Battles for Lansdale, Pennsylvania   **31**

The Battle for Separation   **48**

The Battle Against Bob Jones University   **65**

The Battle Against Tragedy   **71**

The Battle Against New Evangelicalism   **83**

The Battle Against Calvinism   **98**

The Battle Against the Flesh   **108**

The Battle Against the Masonic Lodge   **135**

The Battle Against Arminianism   **149**

Epilogue   **166**

PREFACE

I was a very young believer and had just come through a tough temptation; I asked my pastor if the Christian life gets any easier. I never forgot his answer, "No, but it's one day shorter." With that thought in mind, I stopped looking for the Christian life to get easier, but I'll not stop looking for the coming of Christ.

I believe the soulwinner does much harm to a new believer if he does not teach a good Bible follow-up course to the new believer. I believe there are thousands of new believers who stumble and fall and do the cause of Christ much harm because of ignorance.

When I got saved, I met two dear believers who took me under their wings. Day and night they helped me and loved me. Night after night, Dick and Martha Mitchell taught me and debated with me till I was able to stand on my own two feet, spiritually speaking. I'll never be able to repay my two good friends for teaching me many biblical truths. One of the most important truths was that the Christian life is a war that starts at salvation and ends at death or the Rapture. It's been well over fifty years since Dick and Martha taught me about the battles, and they were right. The battles are not easier, but the end is more than fifty years closer.

Over the years when I have been tempted just to give in a little, I could almost see Dick, who is in heaven now, point that Irish finger with just a tone of anger saying, "Bob Jordan, the battle is not yours to surrender. The battle is the Lord's, and He expects you to be fighting His battle when you die or when He comes for us." So for over fifty years, I've been fighting the Lord's battles. I've never had to look for one, for when one was over, the Devil would create another one.

ACKNOWLEDGMENTS

It is difficult to produce a book without the help of others. With this thought in mind, *I count it all joy to give credit to the many who humbly made good suggestions.*

Our senior pastor and our son, Dr. Timothy Robert Jordan, and the pastoral staff of Calvary Baptist Church.

The Calvary Baptist Theological Seminary staff, headed by Dr. David Burggraff, president.

The information technology staff headed by Mr. Harold Chapin.

Mrs. Evie Gahman, an outstanding believer, wife, and mother of two in full-time service. She is the full-time secretary at Calvary Baptist Theological Seminary. In all her busyness she made time to correct this manuscript.

Mr. John Gahman, who made himself available day and night to help with my computer.

Time would fail me to thank the multitude of faithful members of the Calvary Baptist Church of Lansdale. For they not only made many profitable suggestions but also prayed continuously that I would produce a book that would honor our wonderful Lord.

INTRODUCTION

For some years now, my students and pastoral friends have tried to persuade me to do some writing. I have always believed that God called me to preach, not to write. Over the years I have not felt led to put my thoughts on paper or in a book. Recently all that changed, and I had to allow God to make the change. About ten years ago, I was diagnosed with Parkinson's disease. For the first few years, I hardly knew there was anything wrong, but slowly and surely my body began to change. With all the changes, I have never had one day of pain. Praise the Lord!

Slowly the disease began to attack my voice. A preacher with no voice is like a paperhanger without hands. The doctors gave me no hope of recovering my voice, so I preached as long as I could. Now it is almost impossible to communicate verbally. I spent time with the Lord asking Him what I could do with my life now that I wasn't able to preach anymore. God's direction to me was to get myself busy in the church and do anything I could. In the back of my mind there was still no thought of writing as I recalled that verse in I Corinthians 7:20, "Let every man abide in the same calling wherein he was called."

One day I was sitting in the dentist chair of Dr. Christopher Rohrbach, graduate of Calvary Baptist Theological Seminary. Out of the blue he looked me in the eye and said, "Chief, has it ever occurred to you that the Lord permitted the loss of your voice to get you to write?"

I confess that I was so busy doing what I could do here at the church that writing never occurred to me as something I should be doing. I went to the Lord in prayer once again and believed He was encouraging me to write as well. To my surprise, as I started to put words on paper, I really started to enjoy it. I may never write a good book, but believing it is His will for me, here I go. I only pray that if I ever run ahead of God, He will prevent me from moving forward in any direction that is not His will.

THE BATTLE
FOR MY SOUL—SALVATION

Job 5:7 says, "Yet man is born unto trouble, as the sparks fly upward." I was born in the city of Dayton, Ohio, on September 25, 1925, into a drunken, abusive, unfaithful home. My mother finally forsook all five of her children. My dad very quickly remarried. Since I've gotten saved, I've met many God-honoring stepmothers, but my stepmother was not one of them.

She spent most of the day mocking my two sisters and me by beating and starving us. One day when I was three, one of us did something wrong, so she sent me out to get a switch from one of the bushes. When I brought it to her, she was displeased, so she went out to get a switch from the rosebush. When she was done beating us, we were all bloody. Later that day Margaret, my older sister who was five, said to me, "Let's run away." I did not know what that meant, but it sounded good.

We took turns carrying our little sister, Arlene. Now don't ask me how we did it, but on that day one five-year-old and one three-year-old carried a one-year-old through Dayton. We were looking for our grandparents' home. That we found it had to be of the Lord. Our grandparents took us to court, and the court decided to put us in an orphanage. Shawen Acres was the orphanage where I stayed for almost twelve years.

CHIEF

On the way to the orphanage my social worker, Mrs. Grimes, said to me, "Bobby, at this home you can play." I have never forgotten her name because, I believe, I had never heard the word *play* before.

Shawen Acres was the county orphanage in Dayton. It was composed of twelve cottages arranged in an oval with a main building. Each cottage had a cottage mother and father in it. Each cottage had six bedrooms with four boys or girls in each bedroom. Each bedroom was painted a different color to identify it.

I was placed in cottage number 1 in a green room. I remember standing in the middle of the room feeling like a lost soul when another boy walked up to me and smacked me in the mouth. Of course, I did not understand the situation at all. But I soon learned that there was a pecking order. I learned that you were expected to fight for everything. The bottom boy on the totem pole got all of the dirty jobs, like cleaning, picking up, and being the slave to the "big boy." He also got his food last. I learned that to be the big boy you had to lick the twenty-three below you.

So, to my knowledge, I got my first real goal in life, to become the big boy of cottage number 1. I took a lot of beatings in the next ten years, but when I was thirteen (that's how long it took me to lick twenty-two boys), I became the boy next to the big boy. I remember how proud I was of myself. Only one more boy hindered me from my first life's goal of being the big boy.

It took a year, but every time we got close we fought. Sure enough, one day we fought and he lost. I was now BIG BOY OF COTTAGE 1.

I now had begun to learn that there will always be challenges in life with problems and trials. There was no escaping it. My next goal was to become the big boy of the entire orphanage. That meant I had to fight and beat the nine boys ahead of me. Of course, they were not dumb and knew I was after them.

I tried to pick out the weakest one, but all were tough and it took two years. I had nothing better to do, so I fought on. When I was fifteen, I fought and won. I was sure that now the bands would play and the lights would flash and a Jordan holiday would be declared. But I went back to the drudgery of daily living with no more goals to reach.

I hated school and I was regularly being expelled. In those days you had to repeat your grade until you passed it. I had failed so often I found myself sixteen-and-a-half, and I was still in the sixth grade. The one great thing about the Second World War was that it got me out of the sixth grade. I was always in trouble due to my anger. One day when I was coming home from school a boy jumped on my back and forced me to carry him for about half a mile. I got so mad that I managed to throw him through a plate glass window of a show room.

All the time I was in the orphanage, my father and mother never came to see me or my two sisters although they lived in the same town. Every weekend was visitation, but not for us. I hated being an unknown because of having no family. A terrible hate was growing in my heart. My hate for my stepmother was burning in me, and I began to plan to kill her. How I thank my God that was the only goal I was unsuccessful at reaching, but I came close.

In August of 1942, I was lying on a couch in the green room when my cottage father came running into the room hollering, "Jordan, you are needed to fight in the war with Japan." I had no idea what a war was, but he explained. He told me I would have to go, so he signed me up in the navy. I remember asking him what the navy was because I didn't know. In two weeks I was on a train headed for the Great Lakes Naval Training Station just outside of Chicago. I was told there were 2,700 seventeen-year-olds and one sixteen-and-a-half-year-old on the train, and that was me!

When we arrived, many ugly, loud-mouthed shore patrolmen, who were shouting out a hundred orders, greeted us. One of them pushed me into line, and I said to him, "Who do you think you are?" His reply was that he was a boatswain's mate and that in the navy they were the bosses. I replied that I wanted his job. This gave me my third goal in life, for I would become a boatswain's mate.

CHIEF

I was only there a few days when I got into a fight and got caught. Instead of my lieutenant putting me into the brig (since I liked to fight so much), he told me to fight for him on Friday. I asked who I was going to fight and was told I would be fighting the marines. I asked if that was another name for the Japanese. I thought all servicemen were sailors. He said if I lost the fight I would go to the brig. All of my fighting in the orphanage paid off because I won the fight. Now I had another goal: I wanted to be a champion boxer on the navy boxing team. When I got to the gym, a navy chief who was the boxing coach was waiting for me. He threw a pair of boxing gloves at me and told me to put them on. They were so big that it was like putting on two pillows. He told me the gloves were big to keep me from hurting him. All the time I was fighting in the orphanage I had thought *I was supposed to hurt the other fellow.* I knocked him out and won the fight.

The war was on, so as soon as I completed my boxing training I was shipped to the South Pacific onto the aircraft carrier USS *Cabot.* It wasn't long before we were attacked by the Japanese fleet. For the first time, I saw men die. I began to ask questions like where are they, what has happened to them, and will they ever come back? I was terrified because I had no answers. Aboard our ship was a Southern Baptist chaplain, and in two years I never heard him mention the name of Christ once.

I spent the next two years in the South Pacific under the leadership of Admiral "Bull" Halsey and Admiral Nimitz. The most terrifying experience for me was the Japanese suicide bombers, who would load a plane with explosives to become a huge bomb. The pilot would get all drugged up to fly his plane into our ship. We would see them coming and try to shoot them down before they hit us. Thousands of sailors were killed and millions of dollars lost because of damaged or sunken ships. When you see a plane coming at you, you understand it is either you or him. It is an experience that you never get over and never forget. Even as I write, it is still vivid in my mind.

Mr. Ernie Pyle, probably the most famous war correspondent in World War II, spent time aboard the USS *Cabot*, of which I am a Plank Owner, a sailor who is a member of the original crew of a new ship. He wrote a book about us called *The Iron Lady*. He was killed shortly after leaving the *Cabot*.

We were getting ready for another invasion when over the PA system came the greatest news we had ever heard. We were ordered back to Hawaii. The very next day came sad news that destroyed our good news—our president Franklin D. Roosevelt had died. I'll never forget going under the Golden Gate Bridge, for this meant we were finally home.

As soon as we arrived, my life became one long drinking binge. I realized that I was totally alone. You see, all of the other sailors were going home to a mom and dad. I didn't have a home; I had no place to go. All I had was fighting and drinking.

The war ended, and God had spared me. By now I had a soul filled with hatred and confusion. I had so many questions with no answers. I started drinking heavily, but drink could not take away my confusion. I stole a .45 handgun and took a thirty-day leave to set out to kill my stepmother. I figured God hadn't let me die in the war so that I could kill her. I followed her every day, but each time I had her in a place that I could kill her, she would change her movement. No matter how hard I tried, things didn't work out for me to get her, and then my leave was up. My hitch in the navy was also up, so I re-enlisted for six years, and the navy became my home.

By this time, I had accomplished two more goals. I was now a second-class boatswain's mate, and I had become a middleweight champion boxer in the United States Navy. I did not have any more goals, and without goals I had no meaning to life, so I fought and drank.

I got a new set of orders to go to Philadelphia, Pennsylvania, to catch the USS *Rochester*, a brand-new heavy cruiser. It was a tremendous experience because I was made a first-class boatswain's mate. I also met up with my brother Tom and older sister Grace, who had been raised by uncles instead of the orphanage. Tom was having his two-week reserve cruise on my ship.

My life took on new meaning as I got a new goal. The skipper informed me that since I was the only boatswain's mate with war experience, I would be leader of the First Division. He gave me the special duty of having seventy-two new recruits. That was like giving me a death sentence. I would never be promoted to chief boatswain's mate because every division was graded and promoted based on its efficiency.

The next day my prize team showed up, all seventy-two seventeen-year-olds. I have to admit I was sick to my stomach. I lined them up into four lines and began to threaten them and curse them. I cursed them, their mothers, fathers, and anyone else in their family. Then I got a real shock. While I was cursing them, I looked to my right and believe it or not, one of them was laughing at me. I lost it and grabbed him by the shirt and asked him what was so funny and why he was laughing at me? He replied that it was because he was happy. I almost dropped dead. I decided to hate him and to break him. I gave him every dirty detail, but nothing worked. He still sang, hummed, or whistled.

Then one day he said to me, "Jordan, do you know what you need?" I immediately said I sure did. I needed more money, more booze, and more women. He came back with, "No, you don't; you need the Lord." My reply was cruel and bitter: Why did I need the Lord; He had never done a thing for me. I had no father, no mother, no family, no home, so I never needed Him.

This young sailor's name was Alfred Thomas Forrest, but I thought that was a sissy name so I called him Tim. That name stuck and we later named our first son after him, Timothy Robert Jordan.

The Lord started working on me, and I am sure that someone in Tim Forrest's family was already praying for the loud-mouthed sailor. One night I decided to get a room in a hotel in Philadelphia. I got my liquor and locked myself in my room at the Lorrain Hotel and drank myself into a stupor. I was drunk, and what I tell you is on a police record. I managed to get out of the hotel and go to Litton's Restaurant. With my white sailor's uniform on I crawled on the floor, getting under the tables and lifting them on my back. I caused havoc as dishes and food and people went everywhere. I then left the restaurant and stole an *Inquirer* newspaper truck. I did not know how to use the gears, but I managed to go around City Hall in Philadelphia, stripping all the gears. I woke up in a jail cell. The next morning I faced Judge McDevit, a very strict judge. That morning the Lord was working, for the judge said to me, "Sonny boy, your guardian angel must be watching over you because I am going to let you go." I thought guardian angel, my foot! I went aboard ship thinking I sure had fooled that judge.

One day while Tim Forrest and I were having our daily debates, he handed me a business card with his brother's name and address. His brother had just come from Bob Jones University and wanted to talk to me. I said, "That will be the day; when there is no fire in hell or snow in Alaska, I'll talk to him."

God continued to deal with me. One weekend I went down to Atlantic City, New Jersey, and spent the day drinking. I got my hands on a magnum of champagne and sat down on the boardwalk continuing to drink. It suddenly dawned on me that I could not move and I was petrified. While I was in this helpless state, a strangely dressed man in a full-length raincoat came along. He stopped, set up a box, then put up an umbrella. He had a long beard and in his hand a large ragged book, *The Metaphysical Makeup of the World*. He began to talk in huge words, which none of us listening could understand. I got mad at him and told him to leave or else! He said that most people do not know who they really are. He said if one of us would let him tell us who we really were he would leave. Of course I told him to tell me. He then said, "Well, well, well, we have a sailor who wants to know who he really is." I said I already knew. Then he came closer and said, "I'll tell you, and don't you ever forget it. *You are who you are when you are totally alone.*"

I do not know how long I sat there, but I sat and cried till I couldn't cry anymore. I saw clearly that I had spent my life pretending to be the person I wanted to be and not who I really was. I had created a sailor that was tough, pretentious, successful, and afraid of no one. But with that one sentence he tore off a mask, and I at once saw that it was me that I really hated.

Another experience took place at Orsadies Bar in Philadelphia. I went to my favorite hangout and was sitting at the bar drinking when in walked three young sailors. They were too young to be in the bar in the first place. They weren't in there ten minutes when they became loud and boisterous because they wanted to fight

As I was watching them, something happened to me. I saw myself, and what I saw I hated. What I saw made me sick to my stomach, for I saw three phonies, three blowhards that were deceived, blind, pretentious, and drunk. I turned to the bartender and said, "Jim, do you see that double shot of booze on the bar?" When he answered yes, I told him that it would be the last shot that I would ever drink. He looked puzzled. I didn't know why I said that, but that was over fifty years ago, and I have never touched booze since then.

I went outside of the bar and sat down on the curb. For the longest time I contemplated my life. What was I to do? Where was I to go? My life seemed to have come to its end—with no answers—so I decided to go back to my ship. I reached into my pocket for some trolley fare, and to my complete surprise, there was that business card of Tim's brother, Frank. I did not know what this meant, but I did remember that Tim said I could get a good meal and a warm bed. I also remembered that his brother was religious and wanted to talk to me. I figured that I was much smarter than he was, so I'd go, listen to religion, get a good meal, soft bed, and breakfast the next day, and leave.

I was in for the shock of my life. I took a streetcar to 36 North Sixth Street. I was totally unaware that it was close to midnight. I rang the doorbell and when it opened there stood a man that filled the door. Wow, he was big! Maybe it was the booze. The very first words out of his mouth were "Sailor, where are you going when you die?" What a jerk! I thought for just a moment and said, "Heaven." I had no idea why I said that. He then proceeded to tell me that I was going to hell without Christ. I said, "Buddy, you are a class act. You invite me to your house, and you've got me in hell before I get past the front door."

I was then introduced to his wife, Joy. What a lovely lady, and what a great couple. Her first words were "Are you hungry? Would you like something to eat?" She then went into the kitchen and after what seemed to be a long time, she finally called us to the table. Wow, the table was full. It could not hold anything else. While I was eating, I thought, boy, they are fattening me up for the kill. I ate enough to kill a horse. If they were going to get me, they would get me full. When I was done and pushed myself away from the table, I told Frank that I was ready for him. "Give me your best shot and tell me all about religion."

To my surprise he said, "I don't want to talk about religion." He told me that he wanted to talk about Christ. I wondered what the difference was. So for the next couple of hours, he gave me the gospel for the first time in my life. I have no idea how many nights they invited me back to their home for dinner. I'm sure the neighbors thought I was a new boarder.

One night they said to me, "Bob, our church is having a week of special meetings. Would you consider coming with us?" I knew that sooner or later they would ask me. After refusing them, I thought for sure they would be mean and not want me around. But they did not push me and showed no irritation at all.

As I got on the bus to go back to my ship, I had a war going on inside of me. I said to myself, "Jordan, what a jerk you are. All of your life you have been looking for someone who had peace, happiness, joy, and contentment without getting it out of a whiskey bottle. They won't hurt you, and they are the only two people in this world that have shown you love." You see, I had never been inside a gospel-preaching church in my life and had no idea what went on there.

I got off the bus and went back. I stood outside for a while because I was shaking all over. I was a grown man, and I was terrified to go inside. I finally got up enough nerve to go in and sat down in the back row. If the back row had been full, I would have left. The congregation stood up to sing, and a good usher saw I was a visitor and handed me a hymnbook opened to the right number. The congregation sounded like a whole church full of Franks and Joys singing. I always tell people not to do what I did. The hymn was so beautiful that I tore it out of the hymnbook so that I could sing it back onboard ship. The hymn was "Blessed Assurance."

The preacher began preaching, and the longer he preached, the madder I got. When he finished, I tried to sneak out, but I did not make it. Frank and Joy turned around and saw me, and they began to holler my name. They made a beeline for me and were both crying and hugging me for coming back. I told them very loudly that I would never come back again. Frank and Joy asked what they had done to make me so angry. Joy, with tears running down her face, took my face in her hands and pulled my face to hers until our noses almost touched and said, "Listen to me, Bob Jordan, Frank and I have given you all that we have, and we would do nothing to hurt you. If you plan never to come back, it seems you owe it to us to at least tell us what we did wrong." I said, "You are right; I owe you that at least. You told that preacher I was coming because he preached all about me. You are the only ones that I know in this church, so you had to tell him I was coming."

I was shocked to see them both break out laughing and others were laughing, too. I angrily said, "What's so funny?" Even the pastor was laughing as he told me this was the Holy Spirit convicting me. I understood nothing of this and made up my mind not to come back. However, I came back all six nights! Every night it seemed that the preacher preached the same thing.

He would end the message the same way, asking people to get saved. You must believe that you are a sinner—you must believe as a sinner you are going to hell—you must believe that Christ died and rose again—you must ask Him to save you. But the preacher had another point, and God and I fought about it every night. That point was that you can't save yourself. You can't help Him save you.

Every night as I went to bed I would say to God, "If I can't help You save me, I'll go to hell." I would remind God that He never did a thing for me—no mother, no father, no family, and no hope other than what I did myself. My trouble was that I still did not see myself as lost.

On Friday night, he preached that life and death are in the hand of the Lord. Somewhere in that message he said, "What if God said to you about three o'clock in the morning, you are taking your last breath. How many more breaths could you take?" I forgot it and went back to my ship. But late that night as I was going over what was said, and I wasn't quite awake or quite asleep, the part of the message came to my mind about taking my last breath and how many more I could take. I sat up in my bunk completely wet with sweat, screaming, "NONE, NONE, NONE." The lights went on and all my men wondered what was wrong with me. I told them that there was nothing wrong and to go back to sleep. I was shaking with fright because, for the first time in my life, I knew I was lost and could do nothing about it. I stayed awake for the rest of that night, for I figured that if God tried to take my breath, I'd just hold it. It is amazing how stupid sinners are.

I had made up my mind that for sure I would get saved at the meeting coming up. I was sitting in the church at 4:30 for the 7:30 meeting. Do you know how long it took for the service to start? Everyone was standing around having a good time while I was waiting to get saved. Then it finally started and as I waited for the message, it seemed to me that they sang every song in the hymnbook. It also seemed that they took ten offerings and had about fifteen solos while I was so eager to hear the message and get saved.

Finally, the speaker stood up and asked how many had prayed for him and the services? About a dozen hands went up. He then turned and said to the pastor, "I'm sorry, pastor, I can't preach tonight because your people won't pray." Of course, I was sitting there in complete shock. No message—did he say he wouldn't preach? I asked the person next to me and was told that's what he had said. I went from shock to hot anger. I'd been sitting there for hours and now this. The pastor pleaded with him to preach, so he finally agreed and said that he wouldn't preach a whole message but that it was possible that there was a lost soul there that needed to be saved. He went through his five points and gave an invitation. Wow, at last, but when the singing started, I froze and did not go forward. The invitation was over, and I wasn't saved. As I was leaving, Pastor Pavy must have seen the look of despair on my face. He asked me if something was wrong, and I told him I was too proud to go forward, so I guess I'd just have to go to hell. He took me into his office.

I got the greatest shock of my life. My friend, Tim, who had come with me, said, "I want to get saved, too." I turned and said to him, "Tim, you do not need to get saved; you're good, you're almost perfect, and you are just confused." I turned to the pastor and told him to unconfuse him. But Pastor Pavy said, "Bob, if he thinks he isn't saved, he probably isn't saved." We had a few hot moments and the pastor said, "Bob, let's deal with you first."

He very simply gave me God's plan of salvation. His questions were great. "Bob, do you believe you are a sinner?" I said, "I sure am." "Bob, do you believe that Christ died for you and rose again?" I did not know why, but I really did believe it. "Bob, do you believe that Christ wants to save you?" and I said, "yes." He then asked what I was waiting for and told me to get on my knees and ask Christ to save me. I remember kneeling down in that little office telling God I was a sinner, and I asked Him to save me.

Then Pastor Pavy asked me what had happened. I remember saying, "I asked the Lord to save me." He replied, "Well, did He?" I said, "I hope so," and he hollered at me, "What do you mean you hope so?" I told him that I thought so, and I hoped so because I wanted to be. The pastor said, "Bob, as far as you know, how many lies did Jesus tell?" I answered, "None." Pastor stated that if Christ never lied, then He was not lying now. He said, "If God can't lie, and you asked Him to save you and He didn't, that would make him to be a . . ." I hollered out, "Liar." Now I knew I was saved because I knew that I meant it. Wow! I knew that this was what I had been looking for all of my life.

Then the pastor turned and before he could say a word, Tim informed him that while I was praying, he had prayed and he also knew that he had gotten saved.

The night I got saved I went back to my ship and was so excited I couldn't sleep well. I couldn't wait any longer, so at 4:30 in the morning. I got all of my men up and what a mess they were. Seventy-two drunks were cursing and hollering. I told them to shut up because I had a great story to tell them. "Last night I asked Christ to save me." I fully expected all of them to shout and praise God. But no, there was only dead silence. I repeated the announcement again and after more silence one of them said. "Jug, do you mean to tell us that last night in Philadelphia you got down on your knees and asked God to forgive you and He forgave you for *all* the sins that we know about?" I said, "I sure do, and He also forgave me of the ones you don't know about!"

The next day was Sunday, and I was getting baptized that evening. Pastor Pavy said that he was in real trouble because he had arranged two speaking engagements for the same time in the afternoon. He had a solution for the problem. He would take the one speaking engagement, and I could do the other at the John 5:24 Mission. I told him it was impossible because I did not want to disgrace our Lord. He told me that if I really had gotten saved the night before, I should just tell them how and why I got saved.

I caught a trolley and went to the John 5:24 Mission. At this point, I didn't even own a Bible. I asked the Lord to let me make sense in my speaking. I looked out the window of the trolley and was struck with an idea. I saw a dead tree limb and also a small evergreen tree. I pulled the trolley cord and told the driver to wait. I picked up the dead tree limb, broke off a small piece of evergreen, and jumped back on the trolley.

When I entered the John 5:24 Mission in my sailor suit with no Bible, holding the two tree limbs, the manager of the mission looked stunned. When I told him I was the afternoon speaker, he wanted to know how long I had been saved and was dumbfounded when I told him less than twenty-four hours. He was desperate for a speaker, so he let me do the preaching. The place was full of street people, some I knew from the bars not far from there. When I climbed into the pulpit, I was amazed to see some of my old buddies. I used my dead tree limb as an example of my life before salvation, and the evergreen tree limb as my life since the night before when I got saved. To my surprise, I spoke for thirty minutes, and to my complete joy, sixteen got saved. A year later I had the pleasure of meeting several of them in Bible school studying for the ministry. Sunday evening came, and about a dozen of us were baptized.

Pastor Pavy informed me the night I was saved that I should be baptized, and I told him I would never get baptized. He told me that would be fine if I didn't want to obey the Lord. Just say, "Lord, thank you for saving me, but that is as far as I'm going with you." Wow, did that sting! I told him to prove it from the Bible and I would get baptized. It is dumb to challenge a Baptist preacher to prove immersion from the Scripture. I finally told him that I would be baptized.

All of us got our robes on and lined up behind the baptismal pool. Standing in front of me on the ladies' side was a tall young girl. She informed me that she had been saved two years before but hadn't been baptized yet. The whole group decided to go out for coffee after the service. This young lady and I kept talking, and believe it or not, I later married her. I tell people to obey God after salvation and get baptized, and maybe like me you'll meet your mate there. Her last name was Brooks, mine was Jordan, and now we have twenty-eight drips. We had five children, fifteen grandchildren, and ten great grandchildren. Just think if I had not obeyed the Lord!

One of the rules I had in my navy division was that what my men did ashore was their business, but when they came back to the ship, they were to cause no problems. But now that I was saved, a few of them thought they could do what they wanted, and I would do nothing about it. So after my baptism one of the big mouths came back drunk and started making a ruckus. I told Jim to shut his mouth and get in his rack. He then openly challenged me to a fight. I had the lights turned on and woke them all up telling them, "Guys, listen up! Because I've gotten saved doesn't mean that I've given up leading this division." Before I could stop him, he spit right in my face, and that was a bad mistake. I immediately knocked him cold and sat down and cried. I said to him, "You jerk, look what you made me do." I called my pastor and told him. He assured me that I had not lost my salvation . . . praise the Lord!

MY BATTLE

AS A NEW BELIEVER

My ship was leaving for the Mediterranean Sea two weeks after I was saved. I asked Pastor Russell Pavy what to do since we had a Roman Catholic priest as our chaplain. His advice was to start a Bible study. How? Where? When? What? I didn't even have a Bible. Pastor Pavy gave me a Bible and told me to open it at the black marker and just go from there. You have to remember that I only had a sixth grade education and had never read a book in my life. Now I had to teach a lesson from the Bible, which I had never seen or read before. I told the Lord that I would do it if He would guide me.

I then went to the "Old Man," meaning the captain, and asked him if I could start a Bible study. He said I could as long as I did not proselytize. I couldn't even say that big word, so I said, "OK." I didn't know what it meant, so how could I do such a thing. How dumb I really was.

The captain asked if I was going to proselytize and again I didn't know what he meant, so my answer was no. I then told him I was a Baptist because I was saved in the Lehigh Avenue Baptist Church in Philadelphia. I was given a room and it was announced over the PA system that I would be holding a Bible study for about a half-hour. Our first service lasted three hours. Out of the fifteen hundred men onboard, usually only a dozen sailors would show up for chapel service. There were about two hundred that came out for our study. I had done what Pastor Pavy told me. I started where the black marker was. Matthew 1, verse 1, "The book of the generation of Jesus Christ, the son of David, the son of Abraham. Abraham begat Isaac and Isaac begat Jacob." I was so glad to get to verse 18, "Now the birth of Jesus Christ was on this wise." We all had a good laugh with my reading and stumbling over all those Old Testament names. We went around the room telling each other what we got out of the reading. That Bible study lasted almost six years on the ship, even after I left it. Years later I met two of the men from the Bible study who were teaching at Bob Jones University.

Since my ship was going to ship out to the Mediterranean Sea, the church had a going-away party for us. Several sailors had gotten saved and were with us in the church social hall. I had the privilege of walking Marge Brooks home that night, and we were excited about our love for the Lord. We had wonderful Christian fellowship and decided we would write to each other. It took ten days to get to the Rock of Gibraltar, so we had to number our letters. In letter number 1 I wrote *Marge*, in letter 2 I wrote *Dear Marge*, in letter 3 I wrote *My Dear Marge*, in letter 4 I wrote *My Dearest Marge*, and in letter 10 I wrote, *"Will you marry me?"* It seemed an eternity until I received her letters. Letter 1 said *Bob*, letter 2 said *Dear Bob*, letter 3 said *My Dear Bob*, and letter 4 said *My Dearest Bob*, and about letter 12 she said, *"Yes."*

Once we had passed through the Straits of Gibraltar, we tied up on the Rock of Gibraltar and were able to go ashore. On the ten-day trip from Philadelphia to Gibraltar, about twenty sailors and marines had gotten saved. All of us went ashore to hand out tracts. In one of the streets we met a missionary from England named Willie Houvy, a dentist by trade. He invited all twenty of us to his home for a Bible study and some refreshments.

He was a great speaker and a real blessing. After an hour he invited us into his dining room for the refreshments. We were ashamed and humbled by what we saw and heard. We saw a bare table with no cloth on it and a torn half of a napkin with a piece of bread on it. On the bread was a small amount of jelly to cover half of the bread. There was a small glass of water at each place and none of the glasses matched. What he did and said has burned in my soul for over fifty years. He said, "Silver and gold have I none, but such as I have give I thee." We all stood speechless. He was not ashamed of his poverty, and he didn't apologize for his "little." He acted as though he was serving Christ Himself. In a way he was, and that day I learned a thousand lessons on humility and pride.

I could think only of our blessed Lord saying in Matthew 10:42: "And whosoever shall give to drink unto one of these little ones a cup of cold water only in the name of a disciple, verily I say unto you, he shall in no wise lose his reward."

OUR TRIP TO MALTA

I knew nothing about Malta until I got there. Our ship dropped the anchor, and we could see the beautiful island. Believe me, in this case beauty was only on the surface. As usual, the whole gang of us went out armed with about a thousand gospel tracts. We had started passing them out when a great commotion broke out. The police were everywhere, and in about an hour we were all in jail. Passing out religious literature was against the law. Anyone passing out such literature could be imprisoned for twenty years.

I couldn't believe it. We had passed out over 250 tracts before we got caught. Since we were foreigners and ignorant of the law, we were sent back to our ship. As we were walking back to the dock, one of the sailors said, "Hold it and listen." We could hear voices singing a hymn. "What can wash away my sin? Nothing but the blood of Jesus." So, without any delay our gang of about twenty sailors rushed to the house. When we knocked, all the lights went out, and the singing abruptly stopped. We were so happy to find believers we never considered how this would affect those inside.

A dear mature lady came to the door and we could see she was fearful. But she finally let us in after learning of our problem passing out the tracts. She led us to a very large basement, and to our surprise it was filled with about a hundred servicemen from six different nations. They were having a testimony meeting and, of course, I had never heard anything like it. It lasted all night.

Of all the testimonies I heard that night, I remember only one, and I learned a great lesson I will never forget. It was the testimony of a lieutenant in the Salvation Army. He said, "I have been awe-struck of all the sin God has forgiven you murderers, drug addicts, abusers, drunkards, and some that have forsaken their families. Gentlemen, I thank God for all the sin God saved you out of, but I want you to know I was born and raised in a Christian home. I thank God I was saved *from* such sin."

When I heard that, I got on my knees and said, "Oh, Lord, if I ever have children, let all of my children be able to say I thank God that He saved me from sin and not out of it."

Upon arriving home after our long trip to the Mediterranean Sea, I began courting Marge with whom I had been correspond-ing over the last year. We settled for the twenty-second of January, 1949, as our wedding date. However, Marge's family was not at all happy with the idea of our being together.

I took Pastor Pavy over to Marge's home to ask her mother for-mally for permission to marry Marge. The first half-hour she told me all the bad things that Marge had done, like drinking, smoking, and cursing. I tried to tell her that was before she had gotten saved. When Mrs. Brooks saw she wasn't getting anywhere, she started to go into a trance and call on all her loved ones who had died to come and help her stop this wedding. Pastor Pavy, who had much more experience in what was going on, yelled with a loud voice, "Lady, I smell the smoke of hell fires on your skirt!" Well, this stopped all the spirits, and Mrs. Brooks told us we deserved what we were get-ting. We left with Marge to get our wedding rings. The clown that I was, I tried all the men's wedding bands at my nose instead of my finger. Marge just shook her head, and we both laughed that at least the ordeal of asking permission was over.

Marriage was a hard thing to deal with due to my big salary of $120 a month. After all, I did get room and board free. My fu-ture wife made almost as much as I did but had to turn over to her mother everything but $2.00 a week for car fare and lunch money. Her mother was a widow and couldn't work because she took care of Marge's younger sister, Elizabeth, who was a Down's syndrome child. So, we had little cash for a wedding and honeymoon. Besides our lack of cash, there was the fact that the family did not like Marge's newfound faith in Christ. Her mother was an active member of the Third Spiritualist Church of Philadelphia, never missing going to church, and had no love for the short, cocky, baldheaded sailor coming into their home. They considered me a religious nut.

A dear friend of Marge's let her borrow gowns for an entire wedding party. Our only cost was to have the gowns cleaned and returned after the wedding. My men all had uniforms.

My mother-in-law had a very simple reception at her home but did not invite one person from our church of believers. There were no presents except one from one cousin Franklin Jennings, who felt bad and bought us a bedspread. Our friends took over and gave us the very necessary things. We were able to rent a furnished apartment near the church.

My mother came in from Dayton, Ohio. We met her at the train station. She told us she would wear a red carnation. She was able to stay with Marge but was treated coldly by the family. It was strange to see my mother, who had lived in the same town but never came to see me in the orphanage. We saw her off at her train and went out for our wedding supper. Frank and Joy came by the house to pick us up, and we drove about twenty blocks north to a Howard Johnson's Restaurant. We were pleased to be together where we were loved and wanted. Then we looked at the menu. The cheapest thing was a $3.99 dinner, which was more than half of our weekly food allowance. So we all got out of there fast. We came back to our old neighborhood to Fishers Restaurant, finding fried oysters for only $1.50. We really filled up on Oyster crackers and horseradish. We were then taken back to our honeymoon apartment, where Marge jumped out of the car, grabbing me and dragging me for fear that Frank and Joy would come up to the apartment. She is still teased about doing that.

The next day Frank and Joy came over in their car, and we went to church. We invited them back for a spaghetti dinner. Marge and Frank cooked and acted like a couple of kids, while Joy and I went over the morning church service. After dinner we went back to church.

My entire leave of ten days was given over to my dear pastor, Russ Pavy, for visitation—day and night. After all, we were married now, and I had work for the Lord to do. And after all, it was Pastor Pavy who gave us back the $60.00 I gave him for marrying us. Without it we wouldn't have eaten that week. It was snowing and cold, but I didn't think about my new bride sitting up in the apartment all alone. I was enjoying serving the Lord. Can you imagine a child of God being so stupid as to spend every day and evening going on visitation while on his honeymoon? Even worse, can you imagine your pastor encouraging you to do it and going with you? That was just cold-hearted ignorance, and it reminds me of Romans 10:2: "For I bear them record that they have a zeal of God, but not according to knowledge."

Marge went back to work for Simmons Bedding Company in the billing department. My ship went to Boston. I had to hitchhike to Philadelphia each weekend I wasn't on duty. You really had to be in love to do that in the cold winter. Sometimes it took so long to hitch a ride that by the time I got to Philadelphia I could only stay an hour. Then right back on the road to get back for roll call on Monday morning.

THE BATTLE

TO GET INTO FULL-TIME SERVICE

I managed to get shore duty due to my time in combat and foreign service aboard the *Cabot* and the *Rochester*. The Lord gave me the opportunity to go to a Bible institute in the evenings because my job was skipper of a tugboat in the Philadelphia Navy Yard. It was a long ride, but I could get a bus from our apartment on Broad Street all the way to the Philadelphia Navy Yard. My wife and I went together to the institute. I was able to do part-time pastoral work at the church where I had been saved. Pastor Pavy was now in the Midwest, and Pastor Joseph Muggleworth had become the senior pastor of the Lehigh Avenue Baptist Church.

Because of my incorrect grammar and my over-enthusiastic personality, my pastor and my friends thought I should not go into the ministry but stay in the navy. This became a real disappointment to me. How could I lead so many sailors to Christ and not be good enough or intelligent enough to become a preacher? I thank the Lord for the great verse I came across in II Corinthians 8:12: "For if there be first a willing mind, it is accepted according to that a man hath, and not according to that he hath not." Somehow I knew that the Lord would give me all the tools I would need to get my education to be a full-time preacher of the gospel.

THE BATTLE TO GET INTO FULL-TIME SERVICE

Our oldest daughter, Deborah, was born December 6, 1951. Six weeks later I was assigned to the crew of the USS *Intrepid*, bound for San Francisco. I would not get to see Deborah again until she was two.

In California I was assigned to be the acting chaplain of the USS *Matthews*, a naval cargo ship, because cargo ships are too small for a chaplain. The *Matthews* only had 350 crew members.

I had no idea what a challenge this was going to be. We had no piano, no hymnbooks, no communion trays, and no pulpit. There were several ships in port, so I organized the believers into five raiding parties, giving each party the list of things we needed. It was a complete success, and by 3:00 a.m. all of our needs were met. Our ship pulled out at 7:00 a.m. for Alaska.

The easy part was done, but now I had to be the chaplain. I had to counsel the sailors. There were many problems, and most of them I had never heard or dealt with. I had to lead morning devotions and prepare for Sunday morning and evening messages. The worst thing was that I had never done any of these duties.

I remembered praying, "Lord, I didn't volunteer for this job, so my appointment to this job was Your will for my life."

I started claiming certain verses for the Lord's power and guidance—Jeremiah 33:3 says "Call unto me, and I will answer thee, and shew thee great and mighty things, which thou knowest not."

For Strength—I Chronicles 16:11 says, "Seek the Lord and His strength, seek His face continually."

In Trouble—Psalm 91:15 says, "He shall call upon me, and I will answer him; I will be with him in trouble; I will deliver him, and honour him."

Asking and Receiving—John 14:14 says, "If ye shall ask any thing in my name, I will do it." John 15:7 says, "If ye abide in me, and my words abide in you, ye shall ask what ye will, and it shall be done unto you."

With no Bible education and with almost no Bible knowledge and no example to follow, I launched out into the deep. I had to believe that if God said it, it wasn't my decision to make, change, challenge, or rationalize it. The navy had a saying when you were ordered to do something: *"Yours is not to reason why, yours is but to do or die."*

Before leaving the East Coast, I had applied to get an early discharge so I could enter the ministry. There were four ways to accomplish this, and all of the ways involved a lot of red tape and took much time. But Jeremiah 33:3 says, *"Call unto me, and I will answer thee, and shew thee great and mighty things, which thou knowest not."* I went through my ship's captain—The answer was *no.* I went through my senator—After months of waiting, *no.* I went through the chief of Naval Operations—*no.* I went through the Naval Corporation of Chaplains—The answer was *maybe.*

Praise the Lord! I felt that this was God's answer. So I immediately ran ahead of the Lord and called my wife and told her to sell the furniture because we were going to school.

I was flying high because we were seeing souls saved almost daily. Even our captain and the executive officers had gotten saved. I could hardly wait to get out of the navy. Then the Korean War started, and the president added a year to all enlistments . . . the door was slammed shut! I had to stay in the navy. I began to have a bitter attitude toward the Lord. One dark night at sea the Lord and I had a fight. I remember saying, "Lord, You have called me to preach, and I have to get prepared. I've been accepted into two schools and my furniture has been sold. I do not understand."

Being a new believer, I didn't understand running ahead of the Lord. I did not understand waiting on the Lord. I was totally ignorant of how the Lord works. I found myself blaming God for my own stupidity. I did not understand Isaiah 55:8–9: "For my thoughts are not your thoughts, neither are your ways my ways, saith the Lord. For as the heavens are higher than the earth, so are my ways higher than your ways, and my thoughts than your thoughts."

I remember saying to the Lord on another occasion, "Lord, I have nearly eleven years in now, so I will stay in another nine years and have my retirement when I am thirty-seven years old. Then I will spend the rest of my life serving you."

Having said these things to the Lord, I had real peace about staying in the navy until retirement. We were headed back to Seattle when suddenly I heard my name over the PA. I was to report to the captain on the double. When I arrived on the bridge where he was standing, he said, "Jordan, go below and get your bags packed." My question was short, "Why?" His answer blew me away. He said we were arriving in Seattle in five hours and I was being discharged. I was out of the navy. He said to me, "Go preach!" I told the captain that I had given that up for now and I that I would preach when I retired. His answer was, "Stop playing around with the Lord." I saluted him and went down to pack, thinking when I got off of the ship I would go ashore and re-enlist. But to my shock, when I got to the gangplank, there were waiting for me two of the largest, ugliest, and meanest shore patrol I had ever seen. They not only escorted me off the ship but also marched me right to the train station.

When I arrived in the North Philadelphia Train Station, I stepped off the train and looked down at the platform. I saw a very beautiful little two-year-old girl running toward me screaming, "Daddy, Daddy." I had not seen her since she was six weeks old. She knew me because my dear wife had a large picture of me that she placed in her crib every night and taught her to say, "Daddy." I have never forgotten that scene even though it has been over fifty years.

I got a job at Feilen's meat packing plant working the night shift. I poured myself into studying. I went to three schools at the same time. I registered at the Reformed Episcopal Seminary in the morning and the Philadelphia Bible Institute two nights in the early evenings. Every other minute I studied for my GED. Remember, I only had a sixth-grade education. Working from 11:00 p.m. to 7:00 a.m. at the meat plant, I had very little time for anything else.

HOW GOD LED US TO LANSDALE, PENNSYLVANIA

I managed to give time to our local church Saturdays and Sundays. I led the singing, did the Sunday mission work twice a month, and did street preaching. My wife taught Sunday school and sang in the choir.

In the spring of 1954, while in school and just before the birth of our son Timothy, the director of extension at the school approached me with a request. He wanted me to preach all summer and asked if I would be interested. Certainly I was interested. My question was where and for whom? He said that a Mennonite church in Lansdale, Pennsylvania, needed an interim pastor for the summer and fall. I had never heard of a Mennonite church, so I asked what they believed. He said that they were just like Baptists. Boy, was he wrong! He didn't tell me that they were having a preaching contest. They would hear three young men preach and choose one to stay for the summer. After preaching, we were sent home with a lovely widow for dinner. She informed me that I had won and would be the interim pastor. She told me the reason that I had been chosen was that they had wanted an older, mature man. I found out that evening that I was the youngest candidate. They chose me because I was bald and looked older.

I felt sorry for the poor folks at Grace Mennonite. I believed and preached eternal security of the believer. They didn't believe it. I believed and preached baptism by immersion, and they didn't. I believed that the country had the right to wage war and a policeman to shoot if he had to do so. It must have been a sad summer for the members, but I was enjoying it. Souls were saved almost every week, many joined the church, and some were even baptized.

Sundays were hard with two small children. We had to drive to Lansdale each time there was a service or a special event for the church. But the people came to love the preaching and even the new teaching. We developed real friends in the congregation.

One Sunday just before the service started, three men walked in that didn't belong there any more than I did. They informed me that there was a small, somewhat new Baptist church in Lansdale. That surprised me, for I had been in Lansdale all summer and had never heard of it. They explained that the church had never had a full-time pastor and the part-time pastor would soon be leaving. I informed them that it was impossible for me to do anything until the next June. Then I would be done with all my schooling except for four mornings a week in seminary.

I forgot all about them, but God had not forgotten them or me. One night during classes, that same extension director came to see me. He said, "Bob, I have a problem, and I hope you can help me with it." I said I would try. He informed me that the school evangelist was scheduled to speak in a little Baptist church not far from Philadelphia and had become sick and could not go. They wanted me to come to take his place preaching nightly for one week. I was shocked, and as soon as I could get my breath, I said that he must have the wrong man. No Baptist church except my home church knew I existed. He told me it was a small Baptist church in Lansdale. I remembered those three who had come to Grace Mennonite telling me all about Calvary Baptist Church. I told him that I had midterms and could not give them up. He asked what kind of grades I had. I told him I only got A's. He informed me that I would receive the same for my midterms if I would do this for him. I couldn't believe my ears. I told him, "Sir, you have the right man." I did not see how God could have made it any more plain. The Lord wanted me to be in Lansdale. Wow! That was really great, but I had no idea that my Lord had picked out a permanent place where I would minister about fifty years.

THE WEEK OF MEETINGS

I did not realize that the week of meetings would change my whole life. The meetings started on a Sunday morning, and to the best of my knowledge, a large young boy was the first down the aisle to get saved. His name was Joe DiCandilo and he was nine. During that week, I believe twelve precious souls were saved. That small group was thrilled to tears with the excitement of the meetings.

I recall another event that happened every night following the service. One or more members would approach me and ask me to consider becoming the first full-time pastor of Calvary Baptist Church. Each night I said the same answer, "Please, I love it here, but I am committed to Bible school and seminary and am also serving as visitation pastor at Lehigh Avenue Baptist Church." But they were a persistent bunch who wouldn't take no for an answer. On the last night of the meetings, I gave them a slightly different answer. I informed them that in June of 1955, after graduation from Bible school, I could do my last year of seminary and easily be their pastor. I thought that would settle it and they would look for another man. I got busy back at Lehigh Avenue and left everything in the hands of the Lord.

Over the Christmas holiday, after having conversations with the part-time pastor, Norman Jerome, it was evident to me that the Lord was bringing up the subject of Calvary Baptist in Lansdale.

Then I received a registered letter from Calvary Baptist Church written by the church clerk.

Calvary Baptist Church

Lansdale, PA

Rev. Norman B. Jerome, Pastor

Residence: Center Valley, PA

Phone: Allentown—Hemlock 3-6180

January 16, 1955

Dear Brother Jordan:

I have been delegated as Church Clerk to write you as follows:

At the annual congregational meeting held January 12, 1955, the congregation voted unanimously to approve the official board recommendation, that a call be sent to you to become pastor of the Calvary Baptist Church of Lansdale. We know Pastor Jerome has talked to you concerning this matter, and has told us you feel as though the Lord is leading you to join with us as pastor. We are greatly pleased to hear the Lord is leading you to our Church, and the work that is here for us to do.

Pastor Jerome told us that his last Sunday with us as pastor will be the last Sunday in May, therefore we are praying that the Lord will lead you in being able to take over the first Sunday in June.

On Sunday January 23, you will be with us for the day; we are hoping that you will be able to meet with the official board to go over all necessary details. As you know our Church is small at present, (but growing) and we are looking to the Lord for greater things, and Spiritual growth. As souls are saved, and Christians added to the church, we know it will be a blessing to all of us.

As your responsibility grows with more Christians joining, we feel sure that your salary will grow also. We are praying that we may soon have an answer from you in the affirmative, so that we may announce it to the congregation.

Sincerely yours in Christ,

Lillian B. Johnson (Mrs. Robt.)

Church Clerk

Now how could my wife and I ever have a doubt about being called to Lansdale, Pennsylvania?

The pastorate was God's perfect will for our lives. We agreed to go and started preparing immediately because we only had six months to get everything done. We had to resign from being the youth pastor and visitation pastor of the Lehigh Avenue Baptist Church. I had to be ordained. The day of my ordination council, several people from Lansdale were present to hear and see how their new pastor would do.

At the time of my ordination, our son Tim, who was almost two, was gravely ill. He had been born with a severely inverted breastbone that was crushing his heart (his condition was later fixed with a tremendous chest surgery). The people at the council were very concerned for young Tim. The questions were hard, but none so upsetting as "Where do babies go when they die." I answered hell, and a dear lady jumped up and yelled, "Oh, no," and fainted. In spite of my lack of sensitivity, I was very clear on all the doctrines of the Bible and passed the ordination council. The Lehigh Avenue Baptist Church then ordained me.

We had to go through what seemed an endless round of going-away parties. I had to graduate from the Philadelphia Bible Institute and get my GED. After all that, we were ready to move to Lansdale.

As I was walking down the aisle with the other graduates at the commencement of the Philadelphia Bible Institute, a man on my right side whispered a question. He asked if I was the Jordan going to Lansdale, and I replied, "Yes." He told me he had two friends who had just moved close to the Calvary Baptist Church in Lansdale. He wanted me to make a call on them. He shoved a piece of paper in my hand, which I later read. The names and address on the slip were Steve and Edwinna Buck, whom I visited as soon as I could. They came and joined our church and were dear friends for many years. They now are both in heaven with our Lord Jesus Christ.

On one of my early calls to an apartment close to ours, I found a lovely, sweet couple by the names of Wayne and Roma Schankweiler. Roma had been a day student in the Philadelphia Bible Institute. Roma became our piano player and has served over forty-nine years at Calvary. She is still serving the Lord at Calvary.

Very early on a Saturday morning June 4, 1955, a large truck from Hatfield Meats came down to our home on Harold Street in Philadelphia to move us up to Lansdale. Of course, Harry Woelkers was driving the truck. Harry Woelkers and Hatfield Meats are synonymous terms at Calvary Baptist Church. Hatfield has been very generous to our church for forty-nine years. Many widows, students, and countless others have been blessed by this company and their employees such as Harry Woelkers. We followed the truck in our 1947 Chevy coup, which boiled over three times on the ride to Lansdale. We kept stopping to get water from homes until we reached our apartment on North Broad Street.

The next day, which was Sunday June 5, we had a great attendance of thirty-five people. We were thrilled, as it was my wife's twenty-sixth birthday.

THE BATTLE
FOR LANSDALE, PENNSYLVANIA

The Devil wasted no time to go on the attack our second week in Lansdale. It was about eight o'clock in the morning, and I was in the basement when my wife came running to tell me that we were in real trouble. When I hurriedly approached the front door, standing on the pavement was what appeared to be the entire Lansdale Ministerium. It was a fearful sight. They wanted all of Lansdale to witness their power and authority.

I had never seen so many ministers dressed in black and most with their collars on backwards. I asked, "Who are you, and what do you want?" The spokesman said with real pride, "We represent the Lansdale Ministerium and we will ask the questions, not you." "Who are you?" "Where did you come from?" "On whose authority are you here?" "Why didn't you seek our permission?" "Only we have the authority to grant permission to come and start new churches. We do not need any troublemakers here."

I went from being curious to being downright insulted. I could hardly wait for my turn to speak. I raised my voice, making sure all the neighborhood could hear.

"Gentlemen, I want to thank you for coming. First of all I am an independent, fundamental, separated Baptist. Secondly, I did not seek your approval because you have no authority to grant me anything. Thirdly, I get all of my authority from three sources: *From God Almighty Himself.* God sent His Son, the Lord Jesus Christ, to die for me, to save me, and to send me to preach the Word of God. First Corinthians 1:23 says, 'But we preach Christ crucified, unto the Jews a stumblingblock, and unto the Greeks foolishness.' Second Timothy 4:2 says, 'Preach the word; be instant in season, out of season; reprove, rebuke, exhort with all longsuffering and doctrine.' *From the Bible,* the flawless Word of God. Matthew 28:19–20 says, 'Go ye therefore, and teach all nations, baptizing them in the name of the Father, and of the Son, and of the Holy Ghost: teaching them to observe all things whatsoever I have commanded you: and, lo, I am with you alway, even unto the end of the world.' *From the Calvary Baptist Church of Lansdale.* So you see my authority is God the Father, the Bible, and this local church. All of these are my final authority.

"So gentlemen, God and Calvary Baptist called me, and only they can tell me to leave."

The spokesman finally got his breath and said that I would not last long in Lansdale (I have been here for forty-nine years so far). The spokesman continued that nobody would come to hear me. Several years later I met four of the men from the Ministerium in a restaurant and said to them, "You ought to come some Sunday morning and see all of the Nobodies that are there."

I realized that I was in a war, and I soon realized that the war starts at the new birth and ends at death or the Rapture. I also learned that my greatest enemies, I am sorry to say, came from the inside and not the outside. To my knowledge I have not been asked by a modernist, a liberal, a drunk, a prostitute, a bartender, a drug pusher, or a murderer to compromise what I believe. However, I have been asked to change, slow down, not to be so dogmatic, or give in a little by many former church members and many saved pastors.

The first question my wife asked me after arriving in Lansdale was "What do you want me to do in the church?" I am sorry to say that in most fundamental churches the pastors' wives act as though they are the assistant pastor. Most good pastors marry very talented wives and want to use them in the church. Some can play the piano and organ, while others have great voices and the ability to teach and run the ladies' meetings. One of the major problems with this is that some women in the church get jealous. When the church is very small, a pastor's wife can help more, but as soon as members with talent come into the congregation, it is best to use the talents of others. My answer to my dear wife would shock most pastors and their wives. I told her, "Honey, I want you to do every job in the church that no other woman wants to do." If this answer shocked her, she didn't say so. If my answer disappointed her, she didn't show that either. She completely threw herself into three areas of work. She was my wife, and she really worked hard at it. I'm sure that I was never easy to live with, and my schedule was insane. She was the mother of our children, Deborah, Timothy, Thomas, Diane, and Tedd, and at this she had no equals. She chose to work in the nursery and junior church for thirty years. Did it work? Yes, it sure did, and I believe without boasting or exaggeration that in all of the forty-nine years in Lansdale my wife has never caused a problem in our church. And I believe that the several thousand women who have sat in the pews would emphatically agree with me.

REACHING LANSDALE

As I read II Peter 3:9, "The Lord is not slack concerning His promise, as some men count slackness; but is longsuffering to us-ward, not willing that any should perish, but that all should come to repentance," I discovered God's ordained plan. His plan was that everyone in the world hear the Word of God in his or her own language. Believers should be formed into local churches. It should be their responsibility to evangelize the region around them and send out prepared people to help reach the world.

Second Corinthians 10:16 says, "To preach the gospel in the regions beyond you, and not to boast in another man's line of things made ready to our hand." Every day we fall further behind. We are doing a poor job evangelizing the world and an even poorer job winning the ten miles surrounding our church building. It is so much easier to send money to missionaries than to get out of our comfort zone. The average believer never in his lifetime gives a clear presentation of the gospel to lost neighbors, family, or friends and never asks them to get saved.

The average believer has never read his Bible through in his lifetime. The most believers ever do is to occasionally hand out a tract or invite someone to church. How sad, how pitiful, how disgraceful, how disobedient. Yet in God's house on the Lord's Day we sing, "Ye must be born again." We are not doing the best for the Master. We also sing, "Rescue the perishing," and when was the last time we tried. "Anywhere with Jesus I can safely go," but we are afraid to go next door. "So send I you," but that doesn't mean me.

HOW DO CHURCHES GROW IN AMERICA?

I once heard an evangelist say after much research that there are no more than ten churches in America that are growing by visitation, outreach, and soulwinning. Most churches are not growing and if they are, it is by stealing. They steal other churches' members, and then they brag that they are growing. Let a good church have a split and immediately the spiritual buzzards line up to see how many they can evangelize. And these pastors somehow believe this means that they are a better pastor and a better preacher. Galatians 6:7 says, "Be not deceived; God is not mocked: for whatsoever a man soweth, that shall he also reap." I tried for years to get pastors in a wide area not to take in other pastors' members without first meeting with their pastor, with little success. So I wrote the following tract.

Why and How to Leave a Fundamentalist Church

Many believers change churches every year. It is good when believers leave modernistic churches or dead evangelical churches. However, it is not always good when believers leave fundamental churches to go to other fundamental churches. A believer must consider both the reason for leaving and the manner of leaving one church and joining another.

Why Leave

You seldom hear of a Bible-believer leaving a Bible-believing church over doctrine or biblical issues. The vast majority leave fundamental churches because of personality clashes, lack of spiritual growth, backsliding, or pet peeves. (1) Some leave because they see issues (real or imagined) with which they disagree. (2) Others become discontented because they are not active. (3) Others listen to wrong advisors, and of course, "Birds of a feather flock together." Also, "discontent breeds discontent" (Prov. 6). (4) Still others leave because of family, friends, or hurt feelings.

Why should a believer leave a Bible-believing, fundamental church? (1) You should leave if you are moving out of the area. (2) You should leave if doctrinal heresy enters the church which has not been halted by following Matthew eighteen completely. (3) You should leave if there is proven immorality, which will not be disciplined by the church (I Cor. 5). (4) You should leave if the church no longer practices New Testament Christianity of soul-winning, baptism, adding to the church, exhortation, godly living (Acts 2:40–47).

How to Leave

How do believers usually leave a fundamental church? (1) They leave without ever informing anyone. (2) They often join another fundamental church without ever notifying their former church or pastor. (3) Most never try to settle their problems with the pastor, deacons, Sunday School teachers, or other Christians. (They run from their problem.) (4) Some justify their actions using the following excuses: a) "I don't want to cause a problem"—BUT THEY DO. b) "It won't do any good anyway"—BUT THEY NEVER TRY. c) "I know others who have tried and failed"—BUT THEY CANNOT GIVE YOU THEIR NAMES.

How should a believer leave a fundamental church? (1) When a problem arises, you should always follow Matthew eighteen, to work the problem out personally with the pastor, with deacons, with individuals and with responsible leadership. (2) When a problem arises, you must pray and make certain that you have the biblical instruction concerning the situation. (3) When a problem arises, you should not allow the thought of leaving your church to enter your mind. Always try to correct the problem, not to run from it. (4) When a problem arises, you must follow the procedures of the Word of God and your church constitution. Then, if all other things fail, you may leave. (5) When a problem arises and you must leave, always leave so that you can go back. When you leave, do not gossip; do not backbite; and do not try to split the church. According to Romans 12:19, "Vengeance is mine; I will repay, saith the Lord." If you leave the church, you must leave it alone.

Warnings

A WARNING TO CHURCHES: Often churches and pastors are so anxious to grow that they will take members from anywhere and under almost any condition. Too often they do it with pride, believing that they can do a better job for that Christian than the other pastor and church did. Pastors only fool themselves when they think this.

Every church must have a solid Bible position so that members do not run from one church to another without first settling their problems. Unfortunately, most members bring their old problems with them. Let me suggest some standards. (1) Do not build your church unrighteously with somebody else's blood. (Jer. 22:13) "Woe unto him that buildeth his house by unrighteousness, and his chambers by wrong; that useth his neighbour's service without wages, and giveth him not for his work." (2) Do not build your church upon another man's foundation. (Rom. 15:20) "Yea, so have I strived to preach the gospel, not where Christ was named, lest I should build upon another man's foundation." (3) Do not allow someone to sin against another church or pastor by leaving and bringing their problems to yours. (4) Always talk to the former pastor before you permit such people to join your church. (5) If you do let them join your church, make sure they leave the other church alone. They must not bring other members with them to build your church. (6) Always remember, "Whatsoever a man soweth, that shall he also reap" (Gal. 6:7).

WARNING TO CHURCH MEMBERS: When you become dissatisfied and go to another church, you are doing great damage to yourself and to your family. (1) You fail to settle your own problems. (2) You teach your children that they should run from a disagreement. Before long they will apply this principle to job, marriage, or anything they encounter in life. (3) You are not becoming a strong Christian because you are not following Matthew eighteen. (4) You are becoming a stumbling block (Rom. 14). Remember, whatever you do, you always influence other believers. When you are wrong, you influence them for wrong and you become a stumbling block to them (Rom. 14).

THE BATTLE FOR LANSDALE, PENNSYLVANIA

Dear believer, if you are in a good, independent, soul-winning, separatist church, do not leave. Stay and work out your differences for the Lord's sake, for your children's sake, and for your sake. Dear pastor, please do not take, desire, or solicit members from another independent, soul-winning, separatist church. Remember, "Do unto others as you would have them do unto you."

When I came to Lansdale, I came with what I had gotten from the schools I attended. But I soon learned that I lacked several things that are important to the ministry. I lacked an older friend to pray with and to have fellowship with. I also lacked practical training. I had never served communion, I had never given a public invitation, and I had never baptized a new believer. The first lady I baptized had to show me how to do it. I had never held a deacons' meeting, I had never organized a Sunday school, I had never married a couple, nor had I ever written a church constitution. I felt sorry for my new church as they put up with my trial-and-error efforts. But I praise the Lord that the handful of believers were patient with me and gave me time to learn. That is why years later when the Lord led me to start Calvary Baptist Theological Seminary that my goal was twofold: a biblically sound academic education *with* a practical, *know-how* education.

My wife, our two children, Deborah three and Tim one, and I came to Lansdale after having prayed much. What we lacked in knowledge, we made up for with zeal and deep sincerity. Amen!

My plan was to visit all of the old homes in Lansdale first, then all of the new ones. In those days the Chinese laundry put men's shirts around stiff cardboard when laundering the shirts. I laid out the town on these boards and drew the houses on each street. I knocked on every door in this town. One of the calls I made was on Roland and Lorrain Kerr on Oak Drive, Harleysville. They were surprised about my call because they already had their own church. A few years later the Kerr family was not getting fed in their Lutheran church, remembered my visit, and decided to try Calvary Baptist. Roland later served as a deacon at Calvary and Lorrain helped my wife cooking at Camp Calvary for years.

CHIEF

I started in the older section of the town, and I hit a stone wall. All were in church and not at all interested in another one. I then turned my attention to the new building projects, and I used the shirt boards to draw the entire new building sites in and around Lansdale. To my surprise there were twenty new building sites. I made maps of each area. I would draw a line for the road, then put a line for the drive to a round circle for the new home. When the people moved into the home, I colored the circle and made a call on them.

I tried not to miss anyone, so every Monday morning I would take map #1 and visit everyone who had moved in that week. Almost immediately people started to come to our church. One day I had what I considered a great call. The whole family seemed thrilled and promised to be in church on the Lord's Day. I had told the church to pray for them. But . . . to my great disappointment, they never came. Because they were so excited about coming, I knew something had happened.

Monday first thing I was at their front door. After knocking twice and seeing movement in the house, my suspicions were true. The man finally came to the door and yelled for me to leave and not return. It took a while but I finally got him calmed down enough to say to him, "Jim, what in the world has gone wrong? Last week you were so excited and kind, now this week you are full of anger and threatening."

Jim said that after I had left a lady came to their door representing the Welcome Wagon and all the businesses of Lansdale. She warned them of us and our church. She informed them that we were a cult and all of the pastors of Lansdale agreed; we were a wicked and spiritual threat to all in Lansdale and had no right to be there. First, I was righteously angry and then I felt sorry for these people.

Early the next day, 6:00 a.m. to be exact, I was standing on the front porch of the Welcome Wagon lady. After fifteen hard knocks on her door, I finally got a very sleepy response. She asked who was knocking at her door at this ungodly hour. I told her that I was Pastor E. Robert Jordan, pastor of the Calvary Baptist Church of Lansdale, Pennsylvania, and *we needed to talk then not later.* She threatened to call the police and I told her to go ahead; I wanted every businessman who paid her salary to hear what she had been doing. These businessmen paid her to welcome people to our community, not to promote her church and pastor. They paid her to pass out samples of their goods, not to preach hate about some and love toward others. It took her about one minute to pull her head inside, put on some clothes, and fly down the steps crying. She apologized and I accepted her apology and prayed for her. But the sad part was that we never saw Jim and his family again. As a matter of fact, I never saw the Welcome Wagon lady ever again. I think she must be hiding from me and that incident, which happened forty-nine years ago.

GROWING AND BUILDING IN LANSDALE

Almost everything you can do in life that is good, you can do wrong. You can eat right, but you also can be a glutton. You can sleep for the proper health of the body, but you can become lazy. You can sing in church for the glory of God, or you can sing for the approval of people. You can start a Christian day school to help young people be more prepared to serve the Lord, or you can start a Christian day school so your children can stand out on the soccer team, the basketball team, or the volleyball team. I have seen this happen in several schools. This principle is equally true about growing a church. It can and should be done for the glory of God but most certainly can be done to promote the flesh and have bragging rights at a pastors' conference. Because some have done it wrong in the super church movement and have large congregations, hundreds of saved pastors sit around with their half-empty church, saying, "Woe is me." Using the wrong examples, they give the following excuses for their empty churches, which is more sinful than their laziness.

- God never called me to pastor a large church.
- God knows better than to trust me with too much.
- All large churches are sinful.

- God never ordained a church to be large.
- Real church growth is not scriptural.

There is nothing wrong with a small church, but don't blame it on God. There is nothing wrong with a small church as long as it doesn't stay small. Is it any wonder we are not winning the world to Christ as He commanded us in Matthew 28:19–20? Soulwinning in most Fundamentalist churches is dying or completely dead. When was the last time you heard of a church going door-to-door calling?

The Fundamentalist churches of today are laden down with programs that keep the average member so busy there is no time for the real issues of life, which are family, soulwinning, and personal time to perfect holiness. There is nothing wrong with a few good programs, but we had better decide which ones are good. And we must make sure they are few.

Pastor and people had better learn to say that "horrible" word *no*! New Testament churches did not grow by programs, but by three things:

- A strong doctrinal position.
- A strong preaching on the whole council of God.
- A strong program of visitation.

Our ministry in Lansdale was based primarily around the following:

- Seeking for the lost.
- Building a place of worship for the believers.
- Fighting for what we believe.

As I sat down to write this book, I came across the bulletin for the dedication service of our last building in 1977. Listen to these quotes.

- 1955—Under the pastorate of E. Robert Jordan, the church began to grow.
- 1956—Due to the increase in attendance in church and Sunday school, the congregation voted to purchase the old Grace Mennonite church.

- 1960—The new building on Valley Forge Road was built.
- 1968—Our first large building seating 2,000 was built.
- 1972—A new gymnasium was built.
- 1974—The largest building was built seating 3,300. (This was the last building built under my ministry.)

TROUBLE IN OUR CHURCH

Growing and building does not please the Devil, so during this same period there were three major splits in our church.

The issues were authority—who would lead the church, the pastor or the deacons?—marriage and divorce, and separation.

As time has passed, I have realized that much of the trouble in our church could have been avoided had I been better trained and if I had had an older pastor to lean on. But one thing I was certain of, God had called me to be the pastor and leader of Calvary Baptist, and only He could fire me. There was one critical time in my ministry when I was tempted to give in and compromise. It was when we were still on Mt. Vernon Street and had just dug a hole on Valley Forge Road for our first new church building. The problem was the issue of divorce and remarriage and whether a divorced person could serve in the church in any way.

My position on divorce and remarriage has never changed since I got saved. From the major passages of Matthew 5 and 19 and Romans 7, I believe that marriage is "Until death do us part." I also believe, based on these same passages, that the Lord gives us the exception clause found in Matthew 19:9: "And I say unto you, Whosoever shall put away his wife, except it be for fornication, and shall marry another, committeth adultery: and whoso marrieth her which is put away doth commit adultery."

The deacons saw it another way: their position was no divorce, no exceptions, and no service in the local church. With some reluctance, they would permit divorced people to join the church, but they would allow absolutely no service in God's house. Divorced people could do no Sunday school teaching, no youth work, no choir, and no song leading.

CHIEF

The deacons threw the gauntlet down to me as the pastor. They decreed, "Agree with us or we will have you expelled." That Sunday I was to begin a series on I Corinthians 7 dealing with marriage. When the deacons asked how I was going to preach it, clause or no clause, I told them to be in church to find out for themselves. For five weeks, I expounded on marriage and divorce. Well, I guess to them this sounded like a declaration of war. They immediately called a special meeting to ask me to change my position or be expelled. Of course, the phones were busy and sides were being formed. Ultimatums were given. It was the darkest time of my life. I couldn't sleep. I paced up and down in my office.

I prayed, "Lord, I haven't been in Lansdale very long, and I have spent a lot of time fighting the modernists and liberals, proclaiming them to be wrong. I charged them with being a bunch of hell-bound, Christ-denying leaders leading the blind. Lord, all of Lansdale has heard about our stand and many have gotten saved. Lord, we only have a few divorced people and they love me and will stand by me. Lord, if I give in to the deacons, I will hurt a few, but if I do not give in, all of Lansdale will be mocking and laughing at our church." Now, I did not hear voices, but this thought came to mind, *"Jordan, whose church is this anyway?"* That did it for me. I got off my knees and said, "It's Your church. I will not give in. If we win this battle, that is fine, but if the church splits up, let her blow!"

Just before the special business meeting was held, my wife was informed by one of the deacon's wives to be prepared to leave the parsonage because it was all over for me. By this time, we had two more children, our third child and son, Thomas, born June 6, 1957, and daughter Diane, born July 25, 1958. My wife and children sat in the back of the church for the entire meeting.

The business meeting started with the deacons announcing not one charge, but thirteen. The verse God had given me was Proverbs 20:22, "Say not thou, I will recompense evil; but wait on the Lord, and he shall save thee." So I said nothing. Finally, a member who was not a deacon stood up to say he was sick of hearing this filth about the pastor. He moved that the board of deacons be expelled from the church. All but the deacons voted for the motion. I was in, and they were out. And the meeting was dismissed.

Can you see a young man volunteering for war, believing he is prepared just because he has volunteered? I am sorry to say, but this is how foolish a young man is who believes he is ready for God's army because he has graduated from a Bible college and Fundamentalist seminary. I had, but I still was unprepared.

In the early 1950s, when cooperation was gaining headway in America, I asked Dr. Bob Jones Sr. to come to a very small church in Lansdale to help a very young pastor get ready for the battle. To my genuine surprise, he said yes. It was one of the greatest experiences of my life.

This great giant of the faith was willing to come to such a small place. Well, that dear man preached as though he were preaching to ten thousand and then he took me aside and explained to me how to prepare. He said, "Brother Jordan, the battle will be hot and long and your greatest enemies will be your friends and even members of your own church. You need to start gathering some biblical principles and make them yours." One of my favorite principles of his is "It is never right to do wrong in order to get a chance to do right." Before he left to go back to Bob Jones University, he prayed for me and as he prayed, I also prayed that I might live by and war by good biblical principles.

PRINCIPLES TO LIVE BY

Here are the principles I believe God gave me.

1. You can be right and still be wrong if you have the wrong attitude. Someone once said a truth told with bad intent is the worst lie you could ever invent.

2. When you have a problem, don't look outside of yourself for the solution.

3. Problems do not solve themselves. God and you do.

4. There is nothing wrong with you saying you are wrong, especially if you are.

5. No one is always right, not even me.

6. Don't let your mouth overload your back. Don't make promises or threats you can't back up.

7. Be on time. When you are late, you are saying your time is more important than someone else's.

8. Don't ever forget that the Lord will not lower the wages of sin this year.

9. Do right and leave the results to God.

10. You do not know what is true until you have heard both sides of a story.

11. Never make a decision while you are angry or depressed.

12. Nothing is right because it sounds, feels, or looks right. It is right because the Bible says so.

Another truth that Dr. Bob Jones Sr. taught me was this: "When God and you settle on some standards, remember they are for you, not the whole world. These standards are yours, study them, pray them into your soul, and live by them."

RULES FOR CHILD TRAINING

1. Never correct children in anger. James 1:20 says, "The wrath of man worketh not the righteousness of God."

2. Whichever parent corrects the child should pray with the child afterwards.

3. The child that is being corrected should never be permitted to go from the parent doing the correcting to the parent not doing the correcting.

4. Always make the penalty fit the crime. Look to the Bible—God always does.

5. The parent that sees the wrong should correct the wrong. Don't save correction for the other parent.

6. Ask the child after correction why he was corrected. Many times a child will forget what he did due to fear of being corrected. If he does not know why he was corrected, he will resent the parent.

7. If one parent thinks the other corrected the wrong child or in the wrong way, he should never say so in front of the child.

8. If the parent who has done the correcting sees that he or she has done wrong, that parent must apologize to the entire family because they all know it was an incorrect judgment.

9. Never let other children do in your home what you correct your own children for doing.

10. Never compare one child to another, whether it is in academics or behavior. Never say, "Why aren't you like . . . ?"

11. From the time children are small, have some type of family conference during the week, once a week if possible. The children should be encouraged to give their feelings about the home and all that goes on there, as long as they speak respectfully. I started too late.

TRAINING BELIEVERS

Matthew 28:19–20 says, "Go ye therefore, and teach all nations, baptizing them in the name of the Father, and of the Son, and of the Holy Ghost: teaching them to observe all things whatsoever I have commanded you: and, lo, I am with you alway, even unto the end of the world."

God's plan is short and sweet:

> Seek the lost.
>
> Tell the lost.
>
> Win the lost
>
> Train the new convert.
>
> Teach the saved the Bible for spiritual growth.

Believers need to be trained in soulwinning. They need to know how to answer questions. They need to know not to guess but to ask the pastor for help to find the answers. Many times a person being counseled has a tale of woe about divorce, abuse, stealing from the workplace, adultery, incest, and sometimes even murder. The personal worker must know how to keep a confidence. What a terrible thing to gossip about something a new convert has said in confidence. If the worker is not trained, he is not prepared to do the job.

There are few schools that will teach these things. When was the last time you heard of classes to train nursery workers, to train deacons, and to train children and youth workers?

Many people are put into leadership roles with no training at all. Someone may see something good in a person and recommend him or her for a position because

> he is big,
>
> he is strong,
>
> she is really talented,
>
> he taught in several other churches,
>
> he has teenagers so he will understand,
>
> her dad was a pastor,
>
> they live in our neighborhood,
>
> you can tell by looking that they are a great family,
>
> or he is a doctor, dentist, banker, or in real estate.

Do you get the message? None of these things qualify a believer for service. If a church has a continuous training program, it will produce many workers, and it will cut down on church dropouts.

When it came to training, I had to invent my own plan. I did not know anyone else doing it, although I'm sure others were. I just didn't know who to contact.

Training for visitation. Acts 20:20 says, "And how I kept back nothing that was profitable unto you, but have shewed you, and have taught you publickly, and from house to house." I went door-to-door calling every day. If I found good contacts, I would ask one of our members to call on them. Soon that member saw how easy it was, especially since he already knew their name, where they worked, how many children they had, and where they had previously lived. Then on Sunday the member and I would meet to compare notes. Training soulwinners was the easiest job. Members were thrilled to be used in soulwinning.

THE BATTLE FOR LANSDALE, PENNSYLVANIA

Training young men to become pastors through our Preacher Boy Program. From 1966 to 1996, we had over 310 young men in the program. And of these, over 100 are in full-time ministry to this day.

We started with one young man named John Sminkey. I developed the program as we went along. It was a very simple meeting five mornings a week. We spent time in prayer and I answered all of his questions. I prepared a seminar each day on a variety of subjects. Then we spent three days in hospital calling. After lunch, we went door-to-door calling until 4:30. From six to eight, we did contact calling. We did this for twelve weeks, and then he went back to school. Year by year the program grew in numbers as well as in events and demands.

TRAINING LEADERS

If the pastor is to train the leaders in the church, he needs to know what the qualifications of each leader are. Our son, Dr. Timothy R. Jordan, who is now senior pastor at Calvary, has done a far better job than I did.

He first trains one large group; then he will work through smaller groups to do specific training. Leaders are then encouraged to pair off into even smaller groups and refine the instruction.

There can be no real argument that one of the reasons for failure in our churches is that our pastors have good academic training with no practical training—we are surgeons with no internship. We are pilots with no flight instruction, and we are soldiers with no boot camp training if we have no pastoral internship.

THE BATTLE
FOR SEPARATION

The two most hated words are *salvation* and *separation*. Salvation is hated and avoided by the lost, and separation is hated and avoided by believers. To preach salvation to believers is not smart because they already have it. To preach separation to the lost is wrong because they can't do it. Since separation is for believers, we need to learn it.

The Old Testament has many examples of men who refused to separate from evil. The prophets Balaam and Balak teach us a great lesson. No one can curse God's children. But if he can get God's children to sin, God will judge them. In Numbers 23:8 we read, "How shall I curse, whom God hath not cursed? or how shall I defy, whom the Lord hath not defied?"

Lot, in Genesis 13, separates from Abraham and joins the heathen in Sodom. His choice results in death and loss. In Nehemiah 13, the high priest aligns himself with the enemy, giving the enemy a place in the house of God. Nehemiah demands that they separate. Nehemiah 13:7–9 says, "And I came to Jerusalem, and understood of the evil that Eliashib did for Tobiah, in preparing him a chamber in the courts of the house of God. And it grieved me sore: therefore I cast forth all the household stuff of Tobiah out of the chamber. Then I commanded, and they cleansed the chambers: and thither brought I again the vessels of the house of God, with the meat offering and the frankincense."

The twelve tribes, in Judges 1–2, had problems as soon as they received their portion of the Promised Land and received this warning, found in Deuteronomy 7:2–6:

> And when the Lord thy God shall deliver them before thee; thou shalt smite them, and utterly destroy them; thou shalt make no covenant with them, nor shew mercy unto them: neither shalt thou make marriages with them; thy daughter thou shalt not give unto his son, nor his daughter shalt thou take unto thy son. For they will turn away thy son from following me, that they may serve other gods: so will the anger of the Lord be kindled against you, and destroy thee suddenly. But thus shall ye deal with them; ye shall destroy their altars, and break down their images, and cut down their groves, and burn their graven images with fire. For thou art an holy people unto the Lord thy God: the Lord thy God hath chosen thee to be a special people unto Himself, above all people that are upon the face of the earth.

Note what happened in Judges 1:19: "And the Lord was with Judah; and he drave out the inhabitants of the mountains; *but could not drive out the inhabitants of the valley*, because they had chariots of iron." Judah did not drive the inhabitants out of the valley but dwelt among them. *Neither did Manasseh nor Naphtali.*

Jehoshaphat, a good king, joins ranks with Ahab, an ungodly king, to go to war. They are shamefully defeated. Jehoshaphat returns home in shame. As he approaches Jerusalem, the prophet Jehu meets him with these words, in II Chronicles 19:2, "Shouldest thou help the ungodly, and love them that hate the Lord?"

The New Testament also speaks about separation and shows there is no room for neutrality. Ephesians 5:11 says, "And have *no fellowship* with the unfruitful works of darkness, but rather reprove them." We also read in II Corinthians 6:14–17,

> Be ye not unequally yoked together with unbelievers: for what fellowship hath righteousness with unrighteousness? and what communion hath light with darkness? And what concord hath Christ with Belial? or what part hath he that believeth with an infidel? And what agreement hath the temple of God with

idols? for ye are the temple of the living God; as God hath said, I will dwell in them, and walk in them; and I will be their God, and they shall be my people. Wherefore come out from among them, and be ye separate, saith the Lord, and touch not the unclean thing, and I will receive you.

"Be ye not unequally yoked together" is clear in verse 14. "Wherefore come out from among them" is also very clear in verse 17. *God's logic is brutal.* "What fellowship hath righteousness with unrighteousness? and what communion hath light with darkness? and what concord hath Christ with Belial? or what part hath he that believeth with an infidel? and what agreement hath the temple of God with idols?" *Demas* loved the world. *Peter* at the fire was with the wrong crowd and brought shame and rebuke. Matthew 26:69–74 says,

> Now Peter sat without in the palace: and a damsel came unto him, saying, Thou also wast with Jesus of Galilee. But he denied before them all, saying, I know not what thou sayest. And when he was gone out into the porch, another maid saw him, and said unto them that were there, This fellow was also with Jesus of Nazareth. And again he denied with an oath, I do not know the man. And after a while came unto him they that stood by, and said to Peter, Surely thou also art one of them; for thy speech bewrayeth thee. Then began he to curse and to swear, saying, I know not the man. And immediately the cock crew.

If you run with the skunks, you will smell like one.

The church of Laodicea is described in Revelation 3:14–19:

> And unto the angel of the church of the Laodiceans write; These things saith the Amen, the faithful and true witness, the beginning of the creation of God; I know thy works, that thou art neither cold nor hot: I would thou wert cold or hot. So then because thou art lukewarm, and neither cold nor hot, I will spue thee out of my mouth. Because thou sayest, I am rich, and increased with goods, and have need of nothing; and knowest not that thou art wretched, and miserable, and poor, and blind, and naked: I counsel thee to buy of me gold tried in the fire, that thou mayest be rich; and white raiment, that thou mayest be clothed, and that the shame of thy nakedness do not appear; and anoint thine eyes with eyesalve, that thou mayest see. As many as I love, I rebuke and chasten: be zealous therefore, and repent.

When you mix hot and cold, it becomes lukewarm and makes God sick, and He will spew it out of His mouth. Cooperative evangelists don't believe this. For many years they have demanded and put the lost and the saved together on a platform of preaching the Word of God. Multitudes have gone along with this. After all, doesn't the end justify the means? No, it doesn't!

One of the reasons separation is misunderstood is that there are three kinds of separation, not just one. I believe if you study your Bible carefully, you will see the three kinds: *moral, ecclesiastical,* and *personal.*

MORAL SEPARATION

Moral separation has to do with that which is moral:

> stealing, Aachan
>
> adultery, David
>
> murder, Cain
>
> lying, Ananias and Sapphira
>
> idolatry, Israel
>
> covetousness
>
> gambling, the soldiers at the foot of the cross for Christ's garments
>
> drunkenness

The moral law of God is complete with no room for interpretation. A believer who breaks the moral law of God for his own profit falls into the hands of an insulted God.

God put the Holy Spirit in our hearts to guide us into all truth. John 16:13 says, "Howbeit when he, the Spirit of truth, is come, he will guide you into all truth: for he shall not speak of himself; but whatsoever he shall hear, that shall he speak: and he will shew you things to come." A believer in sin can never say God led him to do it. For example, there is seldom a week that goes by when some girl and guy don't come and ask to be married. Yet when they are asked if they are both saved, they will say that only one of them is saved. The Bible is crystal clear in II Corinthians 6:14: "Be ye not unequally yoked together with unbelievers." "Thou shalt not" *never* means maybe, or later, or pray about it. It always means no. A couple will come and say they have prayed about a sin and they believe that God is leading them to do this or go there and they have His permission to do it. They explain that the reason they are doing this is that it will lead their partner to get saved.

- *Have No Fellowship*—Ephesians 5:11 "And have no fellowship with the unfruitful works of darkness, but rather reprove them."
- *Withdraw Thyself*—II Thessalonians 3:6 "Now we command you, brethren, in the name of our Lord Jesus Christ, that ye withdraw yourselves from every brother that walketh disorderly, and not after the tradition which ye received of us."
- *Have No Company with Them*—II Thessalonians 3:14 "And if any man obey not our word by this epistle, note that man, and have no company with him, that he may be ashamed."
- *Reject Them*—Titus 3:10 "A man that is an heretick after the first and second admonition reject."

ECCLESIASTICAL SEPARATION

Ecclesiastical separation has to do with *church separation* or being involved in an ecumenical organization that promotes cooperation with unbelievers or backslidden brethren in any form.

Take for example Jehoshaphat and Balak in II Chronicles 19:2. "And Jehu the son of Hanani the seer went out to meet him, and said to king Jehoshaphat, Shouldest thou help the ungodly, and love them that hate the Lord? therefore is wrath upon thee from before the Lord."

In Acts 19:9 Paul separates the disciples from the synagogue. "But when divers were hardened, and believed not, but spake evil of that way before the multitude, he departed from them, and separated the disciples, disputing daily in the school of one Tyrannus."

- *Try Them*—I John 4:1 "Beloved, believe not every spirit, but try the spirits, whether they are of God: because many false prophets are gone out into the world."

- *Mark Them*—Romans 16:17 "Now I beseech you, brethren, mark them which cause divisions and offences contrary to the doctrine which ye have learned; and avoid them."
- *Rebuke Them*—Titus 1:13 "This witness is true. Wherefore rebuke them sharply, that they may be sound in the faith."
- *Receive Them Not*— II John 10–11 "If there come any unto you, and bring not this doctrine, receive him not into your house, neither bid him God speed: for he that biddeth him God speed is partaker of his evil deeds."

GOD'S TEN COMMANDMENTS CONCERNING THE BELIEVER'S ATTITUDE TOWARD FALSE TEACHERS

I.   *Beware of Them*—Matthew 7:15 "Beware of false prophets." They are ravenous wolves!

II.   *Watch Out for Them*—II Timothy 4:3–5 "For the time will come when they will not endure sound doctrine. . . . But watch thou." They despise sound doctrine!

III.   *Test Them*—I John 4:1–3 "Try the spirits . . . because many false prophets are gone out into the world . . . and this is that spirit of antichrist." They have the spirit of the Antichrist!

IV.   *Avoid Them*—Romans 16:17–18 "Avoid them. For they that are such serve not our Lord Jesus Christ . . . and by . . . fair speeches deceive the hearts of the simple." They are deceivers of the weak!

V.   *Do Not Receive Them*—II John 10–11 "If there come any unto you, and bring not this doctrine, receive him not into your house, neither bid him God speed: for he that biddeth him God speed is partaker of his evil deeds."

VI.   *Rebuke Them*—Titus 1:10–13, 16 "For there are many . . . deceivers . . . teaching things which they ought not. . . . Wherefore rebuke them sharply. . . . They profess that they know God; but in works they deny him." By their very works they deny God!

VII.   *Withdraw from Them*—I Timothy 6:5 "Perverse disputings of men of corrupt minds, and destitute of the truth . . . from such withdraw thyself." They are devoid of the truth!

VIII. *Have Nothing to Do with Them*—Titus 3:10–11 (Amplified
Bible) "Reject him from your fellowship and have nothing
more to do with him." II Peter 2:1 "There shall be false teachers
. . . who . . . shall bring in damnable heresies." They perpetrate
damnable heresies!

IX. *Prophesy Against Them*—Ezekiel 13:1–5 "And the word of the
Lord came unto me, saying . . . Prophesy against the prophets.
. . . Ye have not gone up into the gaps . . . to stand in the battle
in the day of the Lord." They may turn you into a moral coward
like themselves!

X. *Separate Utterly from Them*—II Corinthians 6:14–18 "What
communion hath light with darkness? And what concord hath
Christ with Belial? or what part hath he that believeth with an
infidel? . . . Wherefore come out from among them, and be ye
separate, saith the Lord." They are the force of darkness and
infidelity!

The Bible never says *stay in*; it says *come out*. The Bible never
says *infiltrate*. But it does say *separate*. Acts 19:9 says, "But when
divers were hardened, and believed not, but spake evil of that way
before the multitude, he departed from them, and separated the
disciples, disputing daily in the school of one Tyrannus." In spite
of all of these commands and warnings, millions of God's children
continue to disobey. Why? Fear of the people. Look at Peter warm-
ing himself at the fire. Look at Peter at Antioch. Listen to Paul in
Hebrews 13:8. "Jesus Christ the same yesterday, and to day, and for
ever." Proverbs 29:25 says, "The fear of man bringeth a snare: but
whoso putteth his trust in the Lord shall be safe." Why do believers
cooperate? It is because of fear, and for popularity, profit, and gain.
A classic example of cooperation and infiltration is the life of Lot.

Genesis 12–19 is the sad story of Abraham and Lot. It is the
story of disobedience and compromise. It is the story of the evil influence a strong believer can have on a weaker brother.

Genesis 11:27–31 gives us Abraham's beginning, his birth, his
father, and his move from Ur of the Chaldees to Haran, where he
grew into manhood. When Abraham's father died, he left for Ca-

naan. Lot went with him, but then the unexpected happened. A severe famine (Gen. 12:10) made Abraham go to Egypt, and Lot went with him. Now for the first time Abraham was out of the will of God. And so was Lot. In verse 4 of chapter 12, note the words, "and Lot went with him." In verse 1 of chapter 13, Abraham left Egypt "and Lot with him."

Abraham had left Egypt but *Egypt had not left him.* He now had Egypt in his house. Hagar, his maid, and Lot, his nephew, were now thinking like Egyptians. God had prospered them with livestock so they needed more space, and Abraham gave Lot his choice. Look at the basis of his choice of land. He chose Sodom and Gomorrah. Genesis 13:10 says, "And Lot lifted up his eyes, and beheld all the plain of Jordan, that it was well watered every where, before the Lord destroyed Sodom and Gomorrah, even as the garden of the Lord, like the land of Egypt, as thou comest unto Zoar." He pitched his tent toward Sodom and soon he was in Sodom. He infiltrated and did not separate.

Lot was in Sodom approximately twenty-five years. What influence did he have? So often people who cooperate and infiltrate use the excuse "I'll just be a silent witness." In chapter 19, angels came from God to destroy Sodom and Gomorrah, the cities of homosexuals. The homosexuals of that city came to Lot to demand the right to have sex with the angels. Lot offered the most ungodly solution in 19:6–8. Where was Lot's so-called silent witness? As a mater of fact, later we see him in the caves of Zoar committing incest with his two daughters and fathering two sons (Gen. 19:19–38), one named Moab and the other Ammon. From these sons came two nations that became the greatest enemies the Jews ever had.

Today folks teach, "Don't talk; just let your light shine. Or let us do a little evil and great good will come thereby. God never called me to witness." All of them should blush with shame!

Because of our church's stands for moral and ecclesiastical separation, we have faced opposition from different groups. We often had to explain our position on separation to our schoolteachers when we confronted them on moral issues. The Ministerium became a constant irritant, hindering us from getting articles published in the local newspaper. We had trouble getting permission to go on door-to-door visitation When we won against the Ministerium on any issue, they would invent another. In fairness to the authorities in Lansdale, they weren't a part of the harassment but treated us fairly at all times. Many have become our friends.

For forty-eight years my church and I have tried to practice biblical separation, but not to get a distinct place in our community, although separation does create one. We didn't do it to brag. We took the stand because it is biblical, and it is completely the will of God. So we did not cooperate with Billy Graham. We did not join the Ministerium. We did not support Campus Crusade, nor did we become a part of Boy Scouts. We did not cooperate with certain mission boards, and we did not take a part in some camping programs. We could not support some colleges, and we did not support Promise Keepers. I could name fifty more groups that we did not cooperate with. Why? Because they all demand the same things; no local church, no baptism, no tithing, no criticism, no division, no discipline, no dress code, no standards in music. The leaders have total control at the top of the organizations.

PERSONAL SEPARATION

The controversy over personal separation has done more damage to local churches and the body of Christ, I believe, than any other doctrine. The old theologians had three words for it: "Things not mentioned." While the moral law was given by specific commands, personal separation is governed by God-given *principles*. I wrote the following tract entitled "What the Bible Says About Questionable Things."

What the Bible Says About Questionable Things

How often have you heard a Christian say, "Can I do this, can I go there, am I allowed to have this? We soon learn as Christians that the Bible does not speak about everything EXPLICITLY, but it does give principles how to govern EVERYTHING THAT COMES INTO YOUR LIFE.

The Bible is not only written in commandments, "Thou shalt not . . ." Exodus 20, "Go ye therefore . . ." Matthew 28:19–20, "Preach the word . . ." II Timothy 4:2, and many other such commandments. The Bible is also written in very explicit principles which govern all of the questionable things that come into our life that are not explicitly governed under a commandment in THE BIBLE.

The worldly or carnal have little or no concern at all about obeying the Lord, and even some of the explicit commandments of "thou shalt" and "thou shalt not" do not bother them, let alone the questionable things. They feel that they have a right to do what they want to do and they will do what pleases them.

Then, how does a godly, dedicated, "I want to obey God" Christians judge questionable things, whether they are right or wrong? Let me suggest at least eleven principles by which the godly Christian can judge everything that comes into his life.

Eleven Principles for Believers to Judge for Themselves All Matters on Questionable Things

DOES IT MAKE ME LOOK, ACT, OR BE WORLDLY? I John 2:15, "Love not the world, neither the things that are in the world. If any man love the world, the love of the Father is not in him. For all that is in the world, the lust of the flesh, and the lust of the eyes, and the pride of life, is not of the Father, but is of the world."

IS THERE ANY DOUBT ABOUT THE THING THAT I WANT TO DO? Romans 14:22–23 "Hast thou faith? Have it to thyself before God. Happy is he that condemneth not himself in that thing which he alloweth. And he that doubteth is damned if he eat, because he eateth not of faith: for whatsoever is not of faith is sin."

AM I BASING IT JUST ON MY FEELINGS? Proverbs 14:12 "There is a way which seemeth right unto a man, but the end thereof are the ways of death."

IS IT ONLY BY MY CONSCIENCE? Titus 1:15 "Unto the pure all things are pure: but unto them that are defiled and unbelieving is nothing pure; but even their mind and conscience is defiled."

DOES IT BUILD ME UP IN THE LORD AND MAKE ME A BETTER BELIEVER? I Corinthians 10:23 "All things are lawful for me, but all things are not expedient: all things are lawful for me, but all things edify not." I Corinthians 6:12 "All things are lawful unto me, but all things are not expedient: all things are lawful for me, but I will not be brought under the power of any."

COULD IT BE A STUMBLING BLOCK TO OTHER BELIEVERS? Romans 14:13 "Let us not therefore judge one another any more: but judge this rather, that no man put a stumbling block or an occasion to fall in his brother's way." I Corinthians 8:9 "But take heed lest by any means this liberty of yours become a stumbling block to them that are weak." I Corinthians 8:13 "Wherefore, if meat make my brother to offend, I will eat no flesh while the world standeth, lest I make my brother to offend."

WILL IT HARM MY BODY? I Corinthians 6:19, 20 "What? know ye not that your body is the temple of the Holy Ghost which is in you, which ye have of God, and ye are not your own? For ye are bought with a price: therefore glorify God in your body, and in your spirit, which are God's."

DOES IT GLORIFY THE LORD? I Corinthians 10:31 "Whether therefore ye eat, or drink, or whatsoever ye do, do all to the glory of God."

CAN I DO IT IN HIS NAME? Colossians 3:17 "And whatsoever ye do in word or deed, do all in the name of the Lord Jesus, giving thanks to God and the Father by him."

HOW DOES IT APPEAR TO OTHERS? I Thessalonians 5:22 "Abstain from all appearance of evil."

DO I WANT TO REAP THIS IN MY CHILDREN'S LIVES? Ephesians 6:4 "And, ye fathers, provoke not your children to wrath: but bring them up in the nurture and admonition of the Lord." Proverbs 22:6 "Train up a child in the way he should go: and when he is old, he will not depart from it." Galatians 6:7, 8 "Be not deceived; God is not mocked: for whatsoever a man soweth, that shall he also reap. For he that soweth to his flesh shall of the flesh reap corruption; but he that soweth to the Spirit shall of the Spirit reap life everlasting." Deuteronomy 5:9 "Thou shalt not bow down thyself unto them, nor serve them: for I the Lord thy God am a jealous God, visiting the iniquity of the fathers upon the children unto the third and fourth generation of them that hate me."

If you really love the Lord, you will want in every way to be a better Christian and to please the Lord. These principles will, I believe, go a long way in answering questions for you regarding questionable things.

The marks of the dedicated believer show up here more than any other place. Now let me show you how personal separation can be used in the wrong way.

A compromising believer wants to justify himself, so he reaches into his bag of tricks and pulls out a verse that definitely deals with personal separation and tries to justify some moral breaking of God's Word. He drinks, smokes, and gambles. To prove it is all right for him, he quotes a principle. He says he is not convicted about his sin or he quotes the Bible, "Let every man be fully persuaded in his own mind."

When you twist the Scripture to your own destruction, you are misquoting. Romans 14:1–5 speaks about the weaker brother who is not certain about what meat to eat or what to do or not to do on certain days. The Bible doesn't say to be fully persuaded that adultery is wrong, that murder is wrong, or that robbery is wrong. It says be fully persuaded about things that the Bible neither condemns nor condones. Because the weak brother does understand that separation is in three areas—moral, ecclesiastical, and personal. The weak brother, the sinning brother, and the excusing brother tend to say that if the Bible does not condemn something, they can do it. No! No! No! The carnal man says that, but the spiritual man says, "Wait a moment—will this thing that I want to do please God? Can it be a stumbling block to the weak or can I do it in the name of Christ? Only then am I free to do it" (I Cor. 10:32).

WHEN AND HOW BELIEVERS SHOULD SEPARATE FROM BELIEVERS

The whole question of "Should a believer separate from a believer?" is a very thorny one in the church of Christ today. There should be absolutely no question among believers about separation from unbelievers; yet we find many of the New Evangelicals denying even this biblical truth. Even a slight acquaintance with the Bible should make these middle-of-the-roaders blush, since the Scriptures are so plain on this. Below are three leaders in New

Evangelicalism that espoused staying in the old apostate denominations or cooperating with them:

> Dr. Donald Grey Barnhouse, *Eternity Magazine*, September 1957, page 9, "If the Voice Magazine is to be fully honest, it must admit that the greatest forces for orthodoxy at work in America today are INSIDE the old denominations."

> Dr. Vernon Grounds, *Christian Life,* March 1956, page 19, "An evangelical can be organizationally separated from all Christ-denying fellowship and yet profitably engage in an exchange of ideas with men who are New Evangelicals. Why not? How else can we bring them into an experience with the Christ who is Truth Incarnate?"

> Dr. Edward John Carnell of Fuller Seminary in his book *The Case for Orthodox Theology*, page 136, "Separation from an existing denomination is justifiable on only two criteria. First, *eviction*: If the believer is evicted, as the apostles were by the Jews, and as the Reformers were by Rome, a new fellowship must be formed. Second, *apostasy*: If a denomination *removes the Gospel* from its creed or confession, or if it leaves the gospel but removes the believer's right to preach it, the believer must justly conclude that the denomination is apostate."

For whatever reason or reasons these men and many others like them justify such disobedience to God's Word, it is still disobedience and God will hold them accountable.

I.   Should Believers Separate from Believers?

The Bible makes it very plain that God demands purity even if it is necessary to separate brother from brother. We find many such separations in the Word of God: "So there was a division among the people because of him" (John 7:43).

Paul and Barnabas—Acts 15:26–40

Men that have hazarded their lives for the name of our Lord Jesus Christ. We have sent therefore Judas and Silas, who shall also tell you the same things by mouth. For it seemed good to the Holy Ghost, and to us, to lay upon you no greater burden than these necessary things; that ye abstain from meats offered to idols, and from blood, and from things strangled, and from fornication: from which if ye keep yourselves, ye shall do well. Fare ye well. So when they were dismissed, they came to Antioch: and when they had gathered the multitude together, they delivered the epistle: which when they had read, they rejoiced for the consolation. And Judas and Silas, being prophets also themselves, exhorted the brethren with many words, and confirmed them. And after they had tarried there a space, they were let go in peace from the brethren unto the apostles. Notwithstanding it pleased Silas to abide there still. Paul also and Barnabas continued in Antioch, teaching and preaching the Word of the Lord, with many others also. And some days after Paul said unto Barnabas, Let us go again and visit our brethren in every city where we have preached the word of the Lord, and see how they do. And Barnabas determined to take with them John, whose surname was Mark. But Paul thought not good to take him with them, who departed from them from Pamphylia, and went not with them to the work. And the contention was so sharp between them, that they departed asunder one from the other: and so Barnabas took Mark, and sailed unto Cyprus; and Paul chose Silas, and departed being recommended by the brethren unto the grace of God.

Paul and the Judaizing party in the church at Jerusalem—Acts 15

Paul and Demas—II Timothy 4:10 "For Demas hath forsaken me, having loved this present world, and is departed unto Thessalonica; Crescens to Galatia, Titus unto Dalmatia."

Luke 12:51 "Suppose ye that I am come to give peace on earth? I tell you, Nay; but rather division."

II. On What Grounds Should a Brother Separate from a Brother?

There is no doubt that many of the believers who separate from believers do so contrary to the Word of God. Many separate because of hurt feelings, because they do not get their own way, because of their own unwillingness to obey the Bible. But all of these reasons fall short of the Word of God. God Himself gives us the only reasons.

Romans 16:17–18—On doctrinal grounds—Dr. Barnhouse in *Eternity Magazine*, September 1957, page 9, says, "The only grounds for separation between believers are moral . . . there is never a hint of separation because of doctrinal differences." But this passage tells us that we are to *mark* them that cause divisions contrary to sound *doctrine* and *avoid* them. The best example of this today is Dr. Billy Graham. Wherever Dr. Graham goes with his cooperative evangelism, he divides believers. The modernists and liberals never split their churches over him; they profit from him. But wherever he goes, there is hatred, anger, division, and confusion among the people of God.

I Corinthians 5:9–13—on moral grounds—Paul lists six moral reasons for separating from brothers:

- Fornicator—they are sexually impure
- Coveter—they are greedy
- Idolater—they put things before God
- Railer—they are abusive, a slanderer
- Drunkard—they drink any amount (Hab. 2:15)
- Extortioner—they take from others, are ravening

According to this passage we are not to be in fellowship with an individual believer or a church that practices or condones immorality. We are not to have company with or eat with such.

II Thessalonians 3:6, 14—Obedience to the Word of God—These verses make it clear that we are to *withdraw* ourselves from brothers who walk disorderly and who do not obey the Bible. If an individual believer or a church walks disorderly and obeys not the Word, we are to withdraw and have no company with them. If they believe or teach or practice things that are contrary to the Bible, we are to separate. A true believer should not be in a church that sprinkles for baptism, that cooperates with the lost for any reason, that tolerates members in lodges, that excuses their disobedience with an unscriptural love, that speaks in so-called tongues, that does not require a regenerate membership, or that deviates on any of the doctrines and practices of the Bible.

III. What Should Be Our Attitude Toward Those from Whom We Separate?

Seldom do believers ever separate and not become bitter enemies. Yet this is exactly what God tells us not to do. Second Thessalonians 3:15 says, "Yet count him not as an enemy, but admonish him as a brother." We are to separate from our brother on scriptural grounds, but you and I are to be sure that in our separation we have a biblical attitude. We are not to *hate* him; we are to admonish him. We are not to treat him as though he were lost. We are to separate that he may be ashamed because of his sin, but we are to still love him. We must say by our talk and lives to him.

- We will not walk with you (Amos 3:3).
- We will not fellowship with you (II Cor. 6:14–18).
- We will not cooperate with you (Paul and Barnabas and Demas).
- We will not hate you (II Thess. 3:15).

We should be willing to receive him back if he is truly repentant. Galatians 6:1 says, "Brethren, if a man be overtaken in a fault, ye which are spiritual, restore such an one in the spirit of meekness; considering thyself, lest thou also be tempted." Paul sets down a principle that we must adhere to: We should be just as willing to receive the expelled brother back as we were to expel him. Seldom can a person go back to a church from which he has separated on scriptural grounds since so few churches ever come back to the Word. There are many individuals who truly repent and return to the Lord. These we should, with open arms, receive back into our church fellowship. Again Paul gives the principle in I Corinthians 5 and II Corinthians 2. A Corinthian believer fell into the sin of immorality. The church did nothing about it, so Paul demanded, on the Word of God, that he be expelled from the congregation (I Cor. 5:2, 5). The believers at Corinth obeyed. Later this believer repented, so Paul again gave instructions to receive him back (II Cor. 2:4–7) and again the Corinthian believers showed their hearts were right by taking him back again.

CHIEF

A believer can separate from another believer, but he must be certain that it is on scriptural grounds, not because of hurt feelings and so forth. He should be sure he has a Christlike attitude in his separation and not forget to be just as willing to restore fellowship as he is to break fellowship.

THE BATTLE

AGAINST BOB JONES UNIVERSITY

When I was a very young believer and had just come through a tough temptation, I asked my pastor, "Does it ever get easier?" I never forgot his answer. He said, "No, but it's one day shorter." With that thought in mind, I've stopped looking for the Christian life to get easier, but I'll not stop looking for the coming of Christ.

I believe the soulwinner does much harm to a new believer if he does not teach a good Bible follow-up course to the new believer. I believe there are thousands of new believers that are falling, stumbling, and doing the cause of Christ much harm because of ignorance.

When I got saved, I met two dear believers, Martha and Dick Mitchell, who took me under their wings and taught me. They debated with me until I was able to stand on my own two feet, spiritually speaking. Dick is in heaven now, but I'll never be able to repay these two good friends for teaching me many truths. One of the most important truths was that the Christian life is a war that starts at salvation and ends at death or the Rapture. It's been well over fifty-five years since Dick and Martha taught me all about the battles of the Christian life, and they were right. The battles are not easier, but the end is more than fifty-five years closer.

CHIEF

Over the years when I have been tempted just to give in a little bit, I could almost hear Dick as he would point that Irish finger and with just a touch of anger say, "Bob Jordan, the battle is not yours to surrender. He expects you to be fighting His battle when you die or when He comes for us."

Of all of the battles I have fought, the one with Bob Jones University was the most unnecessary, most sinful, and most unscriptural. In 1964, we had a young man from our church at BJU. One day I received a call from the student saying that he had been expelled. My obvious question was "Why?" He informed me that he had challenged a professor and was expelled. My first reaction was anger. Proverbs 19:19 says, "A man of great wrath shall suffer punishment: for if thou deliver him, yet thou must do it again." I had gotten only the student's side of the story. Getting only his biased account of what the problem was, I took his side in the situation. (Notice the I, I, and I.) I had not gotten the University's side and did not realize that there was disrespect on the student's side against the professor. Proverbs 18:13 says, "He that answereth a matter before he heareth it, it is folly and shame unto him."

I should have gone to the Lord for guidance and obeyed the Word of God. I didn't do either. I should have called Dr. Bob Jones and made an appointment to see him. I didn't. I should have gotten in my truck and driven to Greenville, South Carolina, and talked to Dr. Bob Jones face to face, but I didn't. I asked myself the question Why? Why? Why? I didn't follow the advice I had given to hundreds of members as they came to me for advice for similar problems. I should have remembered Luke 4:23, "Physician, heal thyself."

My pride got in the way, and I decided I would talk to the president only if an apology was made and the student was reinstated. No apology came, nor was the student reinstated, and immediately I started a war against Bob Jones University. From that time on I could find nothing right or good about the school or its leaders. I searched the periodicals in our library looking for articles that spoke negatively about Bob Jones University. When I found one, I blasted the school, but in spite of my blast a good number of our teenagers chose Bob Jones University. It was the school they wanted to attend for their four years of education. When they came home for the summer, they had to hear their pastor ridicule their school. But, of course, I spent some time assuring them that I loved them. I prayed for them and told them I would help them if they had a need. What a hypocrite I must have been in their eyes!

Then I started doing something unconsciously. I began to compare the doctrinal likeness between Dr. Bob and me. In a message on New Evangelicalism I would say, "Even Bob Jones stands where I stand."

At times I could see we were very much alike doctrinally and morally. His standards were exactly where we stood on issues. In about a year's time, I must have done this eight to ten times. I would say if God or I could get Bob Jones in a locked room, I believe he would repent, and we could be friends. Then I would chuckle in sarcasm; preachers need to be reminded that God is listening.

One day God dropped a bomb on me. It was a Saturday morning, and I was out shopping. As my practice is, I called my wife, Marge, to see if she needed anything before I came home. She said no but I had better call a lady in the church who wanted to talk to me right away. If I had known what she wanted, I would have booked passage to the moon.

When I called, the lady said, "Pastor, did you really mean what you said on Sunday about Dr. Bob Jones?" Without hesitation I said that I sure did. Then she said that something wonderful had happened the night before. Dr. Bob Jones III was in town for a banquet, and when he went to leave, his airplane would not start. He was stuck in the Holiday Inn in Lansdale. Maybe God was giving me a chance to talk to him. My mind exploded, and before I knew what I was doing, I said I would go to see him. When I hung up the phone, I realized what a trap I had put myself into. I must have driven around Lansdale for at least an hour arguing with the Lord. I said, "Lord, I don't think this is from you," when all the time I knew it had to be from Him. I said, "Lord, all this will be a big brawl." "Lord, you know he is just not worth ruining a whole Saturday on."

I had no peace until I said, "Lord, I am sorry, I will go but You need to guide what I do and say."

When I got there, the lady was there. I called Dr. Bob's room and hoped he was not there. But he was not only there but was waiting for me! We sat down and had lunch together, during which time he asked me my position on many doctrines and issues. After lunch he simply said to me, "Brother Jordan, what do you want from me?" I said, "Dr. Bob, I want you to forgive me, for over the years I've said many things against you and have done many things, too. I want you to forgive me of all those things even though I can't name them all because there are so many." He asked again what I wanted from him, and I told him nothing; I only wanted his forgiveness. He said, "I forgive you for all and completely for everything." He then asked for my forgiveness for anything he had done. He had one request. "If you ever have a negative thing to say about Bob Jones University or me, please say it to me." I promised, and we got down on our knees and prayed together. We got up and hugged each other, and we have been complete friends to this day.

From that day I've never had a better friend, and miracles of miracles, our fifth and youngest son, Tedd, who serves with our number two son, Tom, in Glassboro, New Jersey, graduated from Bob Jones University. What a miracle, a Jordan at Bob Jones University!

The man that I thought to be the worst believer in America and my greatest enemy turned out to be my greatest friend!

- Psalm 103:3—"Who forgiveth all thine iniquities; who healeth all thy diseases."
- Psalm 130:4—"But there is forgiveness with thee, that thou mayest be feared."
- Acts 13:38—"Be it known unto you therefore, men and brethren, that through this man is preached unto you the forgiveness of sins."
- Ephesians 4:32—"And be ye kind one to another, tenderhearted, forgiving one another, even as God for Christ's sake hath forgiven you."

When you read these verses, what do they say very loud and clear? *God forgives sins*!

The only one He won't forgive is the one He can't forgive; and that is a lost sinner dying without receiving the Lord Jesus as his or her personal savior.

Along with sin and forgiveness goes another doctrine. God forgives all sin that is covered with the blood of Christ. *But*, He does not promise to take away the results of sin. They are ours for all time, and there are hundreds of illustrations in the Bible and in our lives that show this is true. First Timothy 5:24 says, "Some men's sins are open beforehand, going before to judgment; and some men they follow after."

Remember David in his acts of adultery and murder? The act of his repentance is recorded in Psalm 51. The fact that he was forgiven is also revealed in II Samuel 12:13. Here Nathan the prophet said, "The Lord also hath put away thy sin, thou shall not die." However in the same chapter are listed several results that followed David for the rest of his life. Second Samuel 12:10 states, "The sword shall never depart from thine house." War was in David's house the rest of his life. Verse 11 says, "I will raise up evil against thee out of thine own house." Note in chapter 13 that Amnon, David's son, raped David's daughter, Tamar. Absalom then killed Amnon. God's point is that true forgiveness is real and complete, *but forgiveness does not take away the results of sin.*

This reminds me of a story of folklore. The story goes that a church member went to her pastor and confessed her sin of gossiping. She asked her pastor the question, "How can I get forgiven for gossiping?" The pastor told her to go home and bring him a pillow from her bed. This was in the days when pillows were not filled with foam but chicken feathers. Even though it seemed a strange request, she obeyed him and brought the pillow to him. Then she asked what else she must do to get forgiveness? He told her to tear the pillow at one end, which she did. She asked what else she must do to get forgiveness. He said to go to the bell tower and dump all of the feathers out into the wind. She quickly obeyed and said to the pastor, "What else can I do to be forgiven?" He told her to go outside and gather up all the feathers to which she answered angrily, "That's impossible because by now they are all over the town!" The pastor told her that her sin of gossiping was like those feathers. She could and would be forgiven, *but she couldn't trace how far her gossiping had gone and she couldn't get it all back*!

With this illustration fresh in my mind, I look at my own life with Dr. Bob Jones III. After Dr. Bob and I got down and prayed, I said to him, "Dr. Bob, I did the harm from the pulpit as I so unbiblically criticized you and Bob Jones University. So this Lord's Day, I will report this event to our entire church." To which he said, "Praise the Lord!"

The next Lord's Day I reported this whole event. I was really surprised that hundreds of our folks said, "Amen." After the service, hundreds told me that they were pleased. Many of the new believers were confused and asked that I give them more information, which I willingly did. It sure was a wonderful thing to watch these new believers come to real growth as I taught the truths of forgiveness and restoration.

But all was not well; the result of my sin began to show its ugly head. I started to receive letters and phone calls from pastors, and most of them were my friends of many years. A few, very few, were pleased. Most were sarcastic, saying I had now become a traitor. To some I was no longer a Fundamentalist, and to others I had denied the faith. And still others felt that Bob Jones had cast some kind of spell over me. It hurt because I had led some of them to the Lord and had helped some of them start their churches.

But as much as it hurt, I could not bring myself to be mad at them. As I looked at them, I could see myself in them. I saw that my sin was completely forgiven, and twenty years later I still bear the results of my sin, but *I had gained a brother* (Matt. 18:15).

THE BATTLE

AGAINST TRAGEDY

Webster's *New Collegiate Dictionary* describes tragedy as having a sorrowful or disastrous conclusion that excites terror. The atomic bomb would be an example. No matter who you are or where you are, tragedy will enter your life. Almost no one is spared, whether you are saved or lost; nothing but death stops it.

The Bible says in Job 5:7, "Yet man is born unto trouble, as the sparks fly upward." Job 14:1 says, "Man that is born of a woman is of few days, and full of trouble." Job 14:22 says, "But his flesh upon him shall have pain, and his soul within him shall mourn."

When tragedy strikes, it usually catches us off guard. Before we can get control of ourselves, we are surrounded by fear, terror, and a desire to find an escape.

There are many heart attacks. A call comes in from your neighbor informing you that your child has been hit by a car. The doctor informs you that you are too late—the cancer has progressed too far and he cannot help you. Your mom or your dad has Alzheimer's disease. Your family has gone down with the plane. Your new baby is born with a deadly disease or with a deformity. Your little girl has been snatched off the playground by a pervert. The stock market has dropped out the bottom, and all of your life savings are gone.

You could add another fifty tragedies to this list. They happen daily, only we are almost sure they will not happen to us.

REACTIONS TO TRAGEDY

John 9:31 says, "Now we know that God heareth not sinners: but if any man be a worshipper of God, and doeth his will, him he heareth."

The lost man's reactions

- He is without God and has no hope in the world.
- He cries to a god without ears to hear.
- His best hope is a "shrink."

The carnal believer's reactions

- He calls on a God with ears, but He will not listen. Isaiah 59:1–2 says, "Behold, the Lord's hand is not shortened, that it cannot save; neither his ear heavy, that it cannot hear: but your iniquities have separated between you and your God, and your sins have hid his face from you, that he will not hear."
- God can help but will not. Proverbs 1:25–28 says, "But ye have set at nought all my counsel, and would none of my reproof: I also will laugh at your calamity; I will mock when your fear cometh; when your fear cometh as desolation, and your destruction cometh as a whirlwind; when distress and anguish cometh upon you. Then shall they call upon me, but I will not answer; they shall seek me early, but they shall not find me."
- His hope is in repenting and returning to the Lord; however, he will go through a period of terror, weeping, and sorrow.

Three questions asked by the spiritual believer

- "Lord, are You chastising me for some sin that I have not confessed?" Revelation 3:19 says, "As many as I love, I rebuke and chasten: be zealous therefore, and repent." Proverbs 3:11 says, "My son, despise not the chastening of the Lord; neither be weary of his correction." Psalm 94:12 says, "Blessed is the man whom thou chastenest, O Lord, and teachest him out of thy law." Remember David and Bathsheba in Psalm 51.

- "Lord, are You testing me?" Genesis 22:1 says, "And it came to pass after these things, that God did tempt Abraham." God tested Abraham with the order to offer Isaac as a sacrifice.

- "Lord, are You teaching me?" Psalm 119:67 says, "Before I was afflicted I went astray: but now have I kept thy word." Psalm 119:71 says, "It is good for me that I have been afflicted; that I might learn thy statutes."

THOUGHTS TO HELP IN TIME OF TRAGEDY

God does not create diseases, but He sure can use them.

If God is correcting you for some unconfessed sin, He will show you that sin. Philippians 3:13–15 says,

> Brethren, I count not myself to have apprehended: but this one thing I do, forgetting those things which are behind, and reaching forth unto those things which are before, I press toward the mark for the prize of the high calling of God in Christ Jesus. Let us therefore, as many as be perfect, be thus minded: and if in any thing ye be otherwise minded, *God shall reveal even this unto you.*

A tragedy that comes suddenly and stays only a short time is usually handled well by the spiritual believer.

Depression, discouragement, and feeling sorry for himself will never give the believer victory.

Blaming God will never get even with God.

A believer telling God that he is through with Him won't make God repent and restore what he has lost.

A tragedy will either help or hinder the saved. It all depends to whom he gives control. Romans 6:12–15 says,

> Let not sin therefore reign in your mortal body, that ye should obey it in the lusts thereof. Neither yield ye your members as instruments of unrighteousness unto sin: but yield yourselves unto God, as those that are alive from the dead, and your members as instruments of righteousness unto God. For sin shall not have dominion over you: for ye are not under the law, but under grace. What then? shall we sin, because we are not under the law, but under grace? God forbid.

It really is true that you are not the only one with a tragedy in your life.

Find someone else who has the same tragedy, and compare notes. You just might share something.

GETTING PREPARED FOR TRAGEDY

One day while I was visiting our oldest daughter, Deborah, she said to me, "Daddy, as a nurse I'm concerned about the shaking in your hands. You need to see a neurologist, for you may have Parkinson's disease." I said it couldn't be because I did not have any pain. I have learned after having it these eleven years that in most cases there is no pain associated with Parkinson's disease.

I immediately contacted an outstanding neurologist at the University of Pennsylvania Hospital. After a thorough examination, he confirmed our daughter's suspicion that I had Parkinson's disease. I went on two medications, which I've stayed on for these eleven years. And through the years it has been abundantly clear that I do have Parkinson's.

Everything in my body slowed down. Things I used to do with ease I now have to work at doing. The disease mainly attacked my vocal cords. My speech began to slur, and soon I had to resign from preaching. Preaching was the delight of my life. Then I had to stop using the telephone for I could not be understood. My poor wife has had to become my mouth. Without my wife, I would have no ministry at all. My wife is hard of hearing and I can't talk, so we really make a pair.

If you come by our house, please forgive the loud speaking. We are just trying to get each other's attention. We have invented hand signs, so between the hand signs, facial expressions, and raised voices, we finally found a way to say, "Honey, I love you."

The Dangers of Tragedy

1. You act as though it is a mistake because you really do not want to have it.
2. You tend to feel guilty and ashamed about it.
3. You withdraw from crowds, parties, and family affairs.

4. It's hard to have fellowship when you can't talk.

5. You feel bad as you watch your family and friends taking pity on you and feeling sorry for you.

   Wake up! Thank God you still have family and friends.

   For fifty years I've counseled hundreds of people who were going through tragedy. What did I tell them, and did it work? If it didn't work, then I have failed. But if it did work, then I needed to take my own advice. We need to hear the Word of God. Luke 4:23 says, "And he said unto them, Ye will surely say unto me this proverb, *Physician, heal thyself*: whatsoever we have heard done in Capernaum, do also here in thy country." "Physician, heal thyself" means "Preacher, take your own advice." I've gone back over my records and to my pleasant surprise, if those that I have counseled took the advice and worked at it, it worked. Praise the Lord!

   What was my advice to those going through tragedy?

1. Make sure all of the advice you are getting is biblical.

2. Beware of sins that follow tragedy around—pride, blame, accusing, fault finding, resentment.

3. Instead of foolish complaining and comparing, ask God how you can use this tragedy as a testimony for Him.

4. Stop looking back at what you lost; you can't get it back. Think on what you have not lost. Philippians 3:13 says, "Brethren, I count not myself to have apprehended: but this one thing I do, forgetting those things which are behind, and reaching forth unto those things which are before." Ask your pastor for a nonpaying job. When I was senior pastor, only five people in my thirty-two years ever came to me volunteering themselves. Only five asked me if I had a job they could do in God's house. Make a list yourself; shovel snow, water plants, cut the grass, straighten the auditorium every Monday, wash the windows, vacuum the rooms, clean the kitchen, and do some painting.

5. Get busy, especially for the Lord. There are so many things you can do for the Lord, like visiting the sick and afflicted. You can contact missionaries and visit orphans. I know only three

people who ministered to orphans, yet the Bible says in James 1:27, "Pure religion and undefiled before God and the Father is this, To visit the fatherless and widows in their affliction, and to keep himself unspotted from the world."

6. Complaining about what you have lost gives you a dark, bitter, and morbid life. Some believers spend so much time complaining about what they have lost that they have no time to praise the Lord for what they have left over.

7. Before I contracted Parkinson's disease, my life verse was and still is precious to me—Galatians 6:9, "And let us not be weary in well doing; for in due season we shall reap, if we faint not." But since Parkinson's has come, the Lord has given me another precious life verse, Mark 14:8. In Mark 14:3–8 we read,

> And being in Bethany in the house of Simon the leper, as he sat at meat, there came a woman having an alabaster box of ointment of spikenard very precious; and she brake the box, and poured it on his head. And there were some that had indignation within themselves, and said, Why was this waste of the ointment made? For it might have been sold for more than three hundred pence, and have been given to the poor. And they murmured against her. And Jesus said, Let her alone; why trouble ye her? she hath wrought a good work on me. For ye have the poor with you always, and whensoever ye will ye may do them good: but me ye have not always. *She hath done what she could*: she is come aforehand to anoint my body to the burying.

The Lord will never ask or require you to do what is impossible for you to do. But everything that He does require, He will provide the wherewithal to do it.

> I preached for the best part of fifty years.
> I can't do that anymore!
> I was able to start approximately a hundred churches.
> I can't do that anymore!
> I was able to see many souls get saved.
> I can't do that anymore!
> I used to love to sing hymns.
> I can't do that anymore!

I used to call about 150 pastors at Christmastime to tell them we loved them and had not forgotten them.

I can't do that anymore!

So what should I do? I could cry, but crying will not stop Parkinson's. I could kill myself, but that would destroy my family. That would cause much stumbling among the many pastors I've helped train. I could do what Job did in one of his strong moments—Job 13:15, "Though he slay me, yet will I trust in him: but I will maintain mine own ways before him." Psalm 40:4 says, "Blessed is that man that maketh the Lord his trust." And by God's grace, that is what I am learning to do. I would like to be like Mary and show that *I can do what I can do with all of my might.*

After finding out what I couldn't do, I determined to find out what I could do.

- I couldn't do electrical work, but I could be the electrician's gofor.
- I am not a carpenter, but I could be his helper.
- I can't do any electronics, but I can follow someone around and be his cleanup man.
- I am not much at gardening, but I can dig, haul, plant, and pull weeds.
- I can't install a dropped ceiling, but I can hand up, pick up, and pile up after someone.
- I found that most good craftsmen need a willing cleanup man.
- I found in Scripture a verse that makes me eligible to serve in God's house to work with my hands: II Corinthians 8:12, "For if there be first a willing mind, it is accepted according to that a man hath, and not according to that he hath not."
- I found that by working around the church I met a lot of members in a new way. We became good friends and learned a lot about each other's needs. We found a lot of time to pray together, and it certainly changed our prayer life.

CHIEF

If there is a need, then *no job is too small or too dirty*. Jobs I found that needed a willing believer to perform are

- straightening up the pews after the evening service
- repairing hymnals
- picking up trash outside the building
- setting up Sunday school rooms and other rooms that will be used
- volunteering to drive or pick up missionaries and take the sick to the doctor or hospital
- praying and developing a good prayer list
- visiting the hospital and shut-ins
- cutting the grass
- shoveling the snow
- helping members move
- replacing burned-out bulbs
- mailing letters to missionaries
- folding the Sunday bulletins
- taking a hot meal to a shut-in

So far my advice has been based on human needs and human success in using these suggestions. Now I want to look at a good practical and completely biblical way of meeting tragedy. Look at II Peter 1:4–10:

> Whereby are given unto us exceeding great and precious promises: that by these ye might be partakers of the divine nature, having escaped the corruption that is in the world through lust. And beside this, giving all diligence, add to your faith *virtue*; and to virtue *knowledge*; and to knowledge *temperance*; and to temperance *patience*; and to patience *godliness*; and to godliness *brotherly kindness*; and to brotherly kindness *charity*. For if these things be in you, and abound, they make you that ye shall neither be barren nor unfruitful in the knowledge of our Lord Jesus Christ. But he that lacketh these things is blind, and cannot see afar off, and hath forgotten that he was purged from his old sins. Wherefore the rather, brethren, give diligence to make your calling and election sure: for if ye do these things, *ye shall never fall.*

The first time I ever read the sentence "ye shall never fall," I was speechless. I went to my pastor and he was no help. I wrote letters to several older and more mature men, and they were no help. As a matter of fact, they didn't mean to, but they contradicted each other.

As in time past when I had had a difficult time interpreting a passage, I set aside a period of time to fast and pray seeking God's definition and meaning. I pray that II Peter 1:4–10 will be as much a blessing to you as it has been to me for many years.

It is obvious that II Peter is written to believers. "To them that have obtained like precious faith" (1:1). So Peter in this epistle wants to prepare the believer to live a successful Christian life. As we look at Peter's advice, we need to remember that the Bible says we are to be *a tree that bears fruit.* Psalm 1:3 says, "And he shall be like a tree planted by the rivers of water, that bringeth forth his fruit in his season." *We are to be a field* that needs to be plowed to grow food. *We need to be a soldier* who needs to be dressed in God's armor to fight and gain victory. Ephesians 6:11 says, "Put on the whole armour of God, that ye may be able to stand against the wiles of the devil." *We need to be a good light.* Matthew 5:14 says, "Ye are the light of the world. A city that is set on an hill cannot be hid." *We are a builder that develops a life.* First Corinthians 3:10 says, "According to the grace of God which is given unto me, as a wise masterbuilder, I have laid the foundation, and another buildeth thereon. But let every man take heed how he buildeth thereupon." We are to develop a life that will not fall. We are assured by God Himself that we will never fall.

Now let's work the problem out in reverse order. God says *we shall never fall.* Now be careful; if we are to claim the promise, we are first of all to accept the condition of God's promises. All of God's promises are *surrounded by conditions.* "Whosoever shall call upon the name of the Lord shall be saved." *To be saved* we must call. John 3:16 has the condition of whosoever believes in Him. Matthew 11:28 says, "Come unto me, all ye that labour and are heavy laden, and I will give you rest." *You must come to Him for that rest.* Too often we are so quick to claim the promise that we forget to find out the condition of that promise. We have the promise in II Peter 1:10, but the conditions are in verses 4–9:

> Whereby are given unto us exceeding great and precious promises: that by these ye might be partakers of the divine nature, having escaped the corruption that is in the world through lust. And beside this, giving all diligence, add to your faith virtue; and to virtue knowledge; and to knowledge temperance; and to temperance patience; and to patience godliness; and to godliness brotherly kindness; and to brotherly kindness charity. For if these things be in you, and abound, they make you that ye shall neither be barren nor unfruitful in the knowledge of our Lord Jesus Christ. But he that lacketh these things is blind, and cannot see afar off, and hath forgotten that he was purged from his old sins. Wherefore the rather, brethren, give diligence to make your calling and election sure: for if ye do these thing, *ye shall never fall.*

So what happens when a believer claims a promise and things don't work out? He begins to doubt his faith or to doubt the Word of God. He sees others claim promises, and they get the blessings. When he is not experiencing the blessings, he lives a weak Christian life and is always up and down.

If that's the problem, how do you correct it? You must *first* believe all the promises of God: "In him are yea and in him amen," II Corinthians 1:20. In other words, God has no pets, nor does He show partiality. If we do not receive the benefits of His promises, it is never God's fault.

Let's look at this most wonderful promise in I Corinthians. First we must see ourselves as a builder. Second, the foundation is the Word of God. First Corinthians 3:10–11 says, "According to the grace of God which is given unto me, as a wise masterbuilder, I have laid the foundation, and another buildeth thereon. But let every man take heed how he buildeth thereupon. For other foundation can no man lay than that is laid, which is Jesus Christ." Third, God is going to show the builders when to lay the blocks, what blocks to lay, and just how it is to be done. The builder does not have a choice of blocks.

Give all diligence with urgency to promptly do things in order. You get the sense of the word *diligence* in I Peter 5:8, "Be sober, be vigilant; because your adversary the devil, as a roaring lion, walketh about, seeking whom he may devour." Notice in building that God asks us to add one brick at a time. The word *virtue* means moral excellence. It means to be clean, free from sin and defilement. Second Corinthians 10:5 says, "Casting down imaginations, and every high thing that exalteth itself against the knowledge of God, and bringing into captivity every thought to the obedience of Christ." Add to our faith a clean body and a clean heart. Psalm 24:3–5 says, "Who shall ascend into the hill of the Lord? or who shall stand in His holy place? He that hath clean hands, and a pure heart; who hath not lifted up his soul unto vanity, nor sworn deceitfully. He shall receive the blessing from the Lord, and righteousness from the God of his salvation."

Add to virtue *knowledge*. It should be a growing knowledge. Second Timothy 2:15 says, "Study to shew thyself approved unto God, a workman that needeth not to be ashamed, rightly dividing the word of truth."

Add to knowledge *temperance*, or self-control. First Corinthians 9:27 says, "But I keep under my body, and bring it into subjection: lest that by any means, when I have preached to others, I myself should be a castaway." Joseph is a perfect example of a believer who had control during the temptation by Potiphar's wife.

Add to temperance *patience*.

Add to patience *godliness*. We should be like Him, be with Him, and live for Him.

Add to godliness *brotherly kindness*. Acts 6:15 says, "And all that sat in the council, looking stedfastly on him, saw his face as it had been the face of an angel." First John 2:9–12 says, "He that saith he is in the light, and hateth his brother, is in darkness even until now. He that loveth his brother abideth in the light, and there is none occasion of stumbling in him. But he that hateth his brother is in darkness, and walketh in darkness, and knoweth not whither he goeth, because that darkness hath blinded his eyes. I write unto you, little children, because your sins are forgiven you for his name's sake." First Corinthians 13 is the key to brotherly love.

Add to brotherly love *the love of God.* It is strange to me that the love of God is last: I John 4:20, "If a man say, I love God, and hateth his brother, he is a liar: for he that loveth not his brother whom he hath seen, how can he love God whom he hath not seen?" First John 5:2 says, "By this we know that we love the children of God, when we love God, and keep his commandments." We talk a lot about loving God, but too often it's just so many words. I believe that true love for our Father comes only when we have laid all of the building blocks in God's order.

We see the very same pattern in Ephesians 6:10–18.

- *The promise*—We can stand against the Devil (verse 11). We can quench all of the fiery darts of the wicked (verse 16).
- *The conditions*—"Put on the whole armour of God," (Eph. 6:11). And put it on in order, one piece at a time. When the believer wants revival badly enough to follow God's blueprint, then he will fast and pray and work on these two passages. He will work on them one condition at a time. He will be rewarded with the precious promises of never falling.

If we stand and withstand, (Eph. 6), God will bring fruit and victory even though we are being torn with a great tragedy and unbearable pain. If we want revival and victory, then we must lay the blocks and check our armor every day. Remember, God did not promise that we would not sin. No, God said we will *never* fall. There is a difference.

Let your illness be an example through which the world can see the greatness of your God. The world is dying to see Christ. The very best way for them to see Christ is for them to see how we handle our suffering! Jesus said in Matthew 5:16, "Let your light so shine before men, that they may see your good works, and glorify your Father which is in heaven." Is your light shining when you lose your mate, your children, or your health?

THE BATTLE
AGAINST NEW EVANGELICALISM

I'm sure that the men who put New Evangelicalism together had no dream it would last this long and cover so large an area or become so destructive to true biblical Christianity. New Evangelicalism arose about the same time I came to Lansdale.

A few short weeks after I got saved, my ship pulled out to go to the Mediterranean Sea. My pastor did me a great favor by having me start a Bible study aboard my ship. I only had a sixth grade education. I had never read a book, and my pastor did not have time to instruct me.

Remember, I knew absolutely nothing, so it had to be all of God. I had to get the captain's OK for a place to meet, and my captain gave me all I needed. I had to get the meeting announced over the PA, and it was announced twice as often as I asked it to be. I taught the class for four years.

I knew nothing except "ye must be born again." Everything else came from a daily reading of God's Word and a daily memorization of Scripture. No church or denomination made me a separatist. God did! No church or denomination taught me to be a fundamental—separated—independent—Devil-hating Baptist. God did!

CHIEF

I learned early that the final test for truth is the Bible. Isaiah 8:20 says, "To the law and to the testimony: if they speak not according to this word, it is because there is no light in them." Whenever a new "ism" came along, I held it up to the Bible. When New Evangelicalism came along, I did the same thing and found it wanting.

When I came to Lansdale, the battle over New Evangelicalism had already started. I found it impossible to stay out of the battle very long. Sunday and Wednesday our people would say to me, "Pastor, how about Billy Graham, how about cooperation, how about Charles Fuller?" As a pastor I was driven to the Word for answers. I tried to be fair with these people, so I would call them on the phone or write to ask them where they stood. I asked for tapes, books, and anything else that would make the battle clear.

To my knowledge, I had only one pastor in a wide area who was like-minded, Dr. Clarence Didden, a dear man of God, from Limerick Chapel.

The great tragedy is that there are many pastors who are worried about their salary. Too many are concerned about their popularity, children's education, and retirement. When their people come to them with problems, the pastors become deaf mutes. God have mercy on men who believe all of the Bible yet betray it. I call them "Gutless Wonders." Shame on them.

Listen to some of their excuses: "I just preach the gospel." They had better read Acts 20:32. They say, "God never called me to be a spiritual detective to check on people." Believe it or not, that is what a dean of my school told me. They say, "Soulwinning is the chief end of man, not fighting." Please give me chapter and verse for that. The chief end of man is to know God and to glorify Him forever.

Acts 20:20–32 says,

> And how I kept back nothing that was profitable unto you, but have shewed you, and have taught you publickly, and from house to house, testifying both to the Jews, and also to the Greeks, repentance toward God, and faith toward our Lord Jesus Christ. And now, behold, I go bound in the spirit unto Jerusalem, not knowing the things that shall befall me there: save that the

THE BATTLE AGAINST NEW EVANGELICALISM

Holy Ghost witnesseth in every city, saying that bonds and afflictions abide me. But none of these things move me, neither count I my life dear unto myself, so that I might finish my course with joy, and the ministry, which I have received of the Lord Jesus, to testify the gospel of the grace of God. And now, behold, I know that ye all, among whom I have gone preaching the kingdom of God, shall see my face no more. Wherefore I take you to record this day, that I am pure from the blood of all men. For I have not shunned to declare unto you all the counsel of God. Take heed therefore unto yourselves, and to all the flock, over the which the Holy Ghost hath made you overseers, to feed the church of God, which he hath purchased with his own blood. For I know this, that after my departing shall grievous wolves enter in among you, not sparing the flock. Also of your own selves shall men arise, speaking perverse things, to draw away disciples after them. Therefore watch, and remember, that by the space of three years I ceased not to warn every one night and day with tears. And now, brethren, I commend you to God, and to the word of his grace, which is able to build you up, and to give you an inheritance among all them which are sanctified.

THE HISTORY OF NEW EVANGELICALISM

Dr. Harold Ockenga, who was pastor of the Park Street Congregational Church in Boston and also president of Fuller Theological Seminary, claims to have invented the term *New Evangelical*. In a news release on December 8, 1957 Dr. Ockenga, said,

> The New Evangelicalism is the latest dress of orthodoxy as new-orthodoxy is the latest expression of theological liberalism. New Evangelicalism differs with fundamentalism in its willingness to handle the social problems which fundamentalism evaded. They need to know dichotomy between a personal gospel and the social gospel. The Christian faith is a supernatural personal experience of salvation and a social philosophy. Doctrine and social ethics are Christian disciplines. Fundamentalism abdicated leadership and responsibility in the social realm and thus became impotent to change society or to solve social problems. The New Evangelicalism adheres to all the orthodox teaching of fundamentalism but has evolved a social philosophy.

CHIEF

THE WHY OF NEW EVANGELICALISM

Christian Life, March 1956, carried a lengthy article entitled "Is Evangelical Theology Changing?" in which many of the young theologians of the day gave an eight-point plan that became the cry-word of New Evangelicals.

1. A friendlier attitude towards science
2. A willingness to re-examine the work of the Holy Spirit
3. A more tolerant attitude toward varying views of eschatology
4. A shift away from so-called extreme dispensationalism
5. An increased emphasis on scholarship
6. A more definite recognition of social responsibility
7. A reopening of the subject of biblical inspiration
8. A growing willingness of evangelical theologians to converse with liberal theologians
   a. The displeasure of narrowness of Fundamentalism
   b. A desire for recognition from liberals and modernists
   c. A new neutralism
   d. A desire to make the cross nonoffensive
   e. A hatred for separation

A New Evangelical is very difficult to describe because New Evangelicalism is a mood, a philosophy, an unwritten theology ascribed. We will try in these next few paragraphs to give a definition of those who hold to New Evangelicalism.

This mood of New Evangelicalism could be described as an attitude of toleration of evil and compromise, of being tired of fighting and desiring peace at the price of purity.

Not every New Evangelical holds to all eight original points of New Evangelicalism, but one thing is true about every New Evangelical. Although many of them will not deny the inerrancy of the Bible, and they will not ascribe to a more friendly attitude toward science, they have accepted the new mood of neutralism, of togetherness, of cooperation, of toleration of evil.

THE BATTLE AGAINST NEW EVANGELICALISM

THE GOALS OF NEW EVANGELICALISM

The goals of New Evangelicalism set down by some of their leaders should be noted by those who are the rank-and-file church members.

1. No separation, but *infiltration*. Dr. Ockenga says, "The New Evangelicalism has changed its strategy from one of *separation* to one of *infiltration*. Instead of static front battle, the new theological war is one of movement. Instead of attack upon error, the New Evangelical proclaims the great historic doctrines of Christianity."

2. To be totally positive and never preach anything negative, unless of course, it is against the Fundamentalist and the Separatist.

3. John Edward Carnell in his book *The Case for Orthodox Theology* lists the reasons that a man should leave a denomination:

    a. If the denomination changes the doctrinal statement in writing.

    b. If a person is expelled.

4. Mass evangelism with the cooperation of, and in the realm of, the established denominations.

THE SCOPE OF NEW EVANGELICALISM

The average Christian who knows anything at all about New Evangelicalism is duped into believing that New Evangelicalism has to do only with cooperative evangelism, with Billy Graham, and so forth. This, of course, is not true. The scope of New Evangelicalism begins in education, where the minds of young men and women can be captured, especially those who are going to hold university positions, seminary positions, and pastoral positions. Then it extends itself to literature, to evangelism, to churches, and to so many other areas. We have seen it with its ties to the National Council of Churches, its theology, and on the mission field, where it is now having its greatest success. We have to understand that this is not a disease that is localized to evangelism. This is a disease that is corrupting the entire church.

NEW EVANGELICALISM IN EVANGELISM

To produce this attitude of surrender and toleration toward evil to the common people, it was necessary to find a plan and a program that would infiltrate the liberal church, the middle-of-the-road church, and the fundamental church, and to get the common man extremely interested in the new mood of New Evangelicalism without him even knowing that he was interested in it. This was done through cooperative evangelism, and mainly through Dr. Billy Graham, although not exclusively. Many other evangelists around the country now participate in and believe in cooperative evangelism.

Doubtless, Billy Graham's position is legend as far as his methods are concerned and what he has done, starting in Los Angeles to his present worldwide status. We have seen the terrible damage as far as the church of Jesus Christ is concerned.

- His plan is worldwide evangelism.
- His method is cooperation between the Modernists and Fundamentalists in evangelism.
- He will go anyplace and preach the gospel to anybody. This, of course, is not true. He will not go to a fundamental group to preach the gospel there; he will do it only if the Fundamentalist will cooperate with evil.
- Billy Graham succeeded in his mass evangelism with Madison Avenue publicity and advertisements. He has done something that no one else has ever succeeded in doing and that is to make the Fundamentalists believe that the end justifies the means. Many hundreds of Fundamentalists who previously held the biblical position of separation were won over to one of the tenets of New Evangelicalism, that is, a *friendlier attitude toward the liberal* and cooperation with evil because souls were going to be saved.

NEW EVANGELICALISM IN THE CHURCHES

Once churches begin to cooperate with Billy Graham, these same churches, who prior to their cooperation stood against the liberal churches of their community, now began to cooperate with the liberal churches.

The one thing so desperately missing in many so-called Evangelical or Fundamentalist churches is *preaching against sins.* This, of course, has to follow. If they are going to cooperate with drunkards, liars, thieves, apostates, and so forth, then how in the world can the pastor preach against sin?

The pastor's message becomes one of devotion, one of missions, one of worship and service, and one of peace. While the pastor preaches evangelism, he seldom sees people get saved.

The great hypocrisy in the churches today is that they are no longer preaching against evil, no longer warning the flock, and no longer preaching real revival. First Peter 5:2–4 says, "Feed the flock of God which is among you, taking the oversight thereof, not by constraint, but willingly; not for filthy lucre, but of a ready mind; neither as being lords over God's heritage, but being ensamples to the flock. And when the chief Shepherd shall appear, ye shall receive a crown of glory that fadeth not away." The great emphasis is now on missions. Churches will spend hundreds of thousands of dollars on programs to promote missions and thousands of dollars more to send missionaries out to the four corners of the world to

- evangelize,
- build new churches, and
- do the whole work of God.

And yet, that very same church seldom sees a soul saved, never starts a new church, and is not doing the work of God.

Truly, New Evangelicalism has destroyed the fire in the church and has caused the church to become the church of Laodicea, neither hot nor cold.

WHAT WAS THEIR PROPOSAL?
EIGHT POINTS TO HELP THE CHURCH SURVIVE

Point one—A friendly attitude toward science. This throws open the battle for Creation to be challenged. Maybe God did not create the world in six literal days. Maybe the days of Genesis were long periods of time. Theistic evolution says that God did create the world, but He used evolution as His means.

Point two—A willingness to re-examine the work of the Holy Spirit. Out of this betrayal, the modern-day Charismatic movement was born with visions and dreams. Charismatics desired everyone to be healthy, wealthy, and wise. Roman Catholics, Baptists, Lutherans, Methodists were all together and all speaking in tongues. Some say that when they see a great crowd hugging and kissing, the kingdom is coming to earth. Churches are packed to have the experience of seeing, healing, and feeling. People want to experience emotion.

Point three—A more tolerant attitude toward varying views of eschatology. Since the beginning of New Evangelicalism, there has been a relentless attack on the coming of Christ. Is Christ coming before the Tribulation, in the middle of the Tribulation, or at the end of the Tribulation, making the church go through the Tribulation? Is the kingdom of God on earth now? Is the next event the coming of Christ or the end of the world? New Evangelicals have done a good job in making this event totally confusing. This is one of the many reasons I stand against New Evangelicalism loud and clear. Since day one I have stood for the imminent, premillennial, pretribulation coming of Christ without apology. Amen!

Point four—A drift away from so-called extreme dispensationalism. This point is being bombarded by the New Evangelicals and reformed theologians. Hyper Calvinists and others bring Israel and the church together to be one and the same. So the church replaces Israel and assumes all of Israel's covenants and promises. This is complete baloney. New Evangelicals credit themselves as great thinkers. They think they can think beyond God. Israel *was, and is, and shall be God's holy choice.* Whoever touches Israel touches God. The promises of God for Israel are for Israel forever. And the promises of God for the church are for the church forever.

Point five—An increasing emphasis on scholarship. There is nothing wrong with scholarship, but scholarship for scholarship's sake is madness. What are their reasons for their PhDs? Do you want to hear a mouthful? Dr. Cornelius Van Til in an article wrote, "To present the important full implication of the Gospel, requires a body of men who are trained in the sciences and in philosophy and who fathom the significance of the Christian religion for these fields." Whatever happened to II Corinthians 11:3? "But I fear, lest by any means, as the serpent beguiled Eve through his subtilty, so your minds should be corrupted from the simplicity that is in Christ." And whatever happened to I Corinthians 2:1–5? "And I, brethren, when I came to you, came not with excellency of speech or of wisdom, declaring unto you the testimony of God. For I determined not to know any thing among you, save Jesus Christ, and him crucified. And I was with you in weakness, and in fear, and in much trembling. And my speech and my preaching was not with enticing words of man's wisdom, but in demonstration of the Spirit and of power: that your faith should not stand in the wisdom of men, but in the power of God." How much plainer can God make it? We need to heed God's warning. First Corinthians 8:1 says, "Now as touching things offered unto idols, we know that we all have knowledge. Knowledge puffeth up, but charity edifieth."

Point six—A more definite recognition of social responsibility. These men are looking for something that our Savior and Paul never did. We are not here to save the material earth, and we can't find a social program in the Bible to do so. *Wait a minute*—didn't Christ feed the poor, didn't believers take offerings to help the poor, didn't Christ heal the sick? Wasn't Christ a compassionate person, and didn't the church care for widows? The answer is yes a thousand times, but these acts of compassion were by-products. The main person is Christ, and the main message is salvation, and the main goal is to glorify God by winning the lost to Christ. The New Evangelicals play right into the hands of the liberals. Don't talk; just live. It is so much easier to hand out funds and clothes. It is also so much easier to collect glasses for the needy, fight drugs by giving addicts sterile needles so they won't get diseases, and feed the homeless.

I am not against social programs, but a person doesn't need to join forces with liberals or modernists to get the job done. Even the church needs to take heed that the programs do not become an end in themselves. Church members find it easier to get involved in social programs than being faithful in attendance and prayer services or making sure that their tithes and offerings are given systematically.

The Scriptures teach us that as we go we should make disciples. I believe Fundamentalist believers should do the same. As you go to work, go for the Lord and be aware of the lost and the needy. As you go shopping, as you go on vacation, or visit the hospital, or see the mailman, or get gas, be a witness for Jesus Christ. We need balance in our lives, and the only way to have balance is to keep Christ predominant in our daily living.

Point seven—A reopening of the subject of biblical inspiration of the Bible. What does inspiration mean? Give a definition. Why reopen a subject that is settled except for the New Evangelicals? Do we open with modernists or liberals? Between whom do the New Evangelicals want to build bridges? The liberals and New Evangelicals must be willing to give a little here and a little there. But it seems that it is always the liberals who win. I'm sure this sounds simplistic to the New Evangelical, but that's the way it should be. From the beginning we have stood for the verbal, plenary inspiration of the Bible. The Bible is without error in the original manuscript, so we have no need as the New Evangelicals do to reopen inspiration.

Point eight—A growing willingness of evangelical theologians to converse with liberal theologians. God in the Bible has clearly defined the condition of the lost man.

1. Man is spiritually dead. Ephesians 2:1, "And you hath he quickened, who were dead in trespasses and sins."
2. Man is spiritually blind. II Corinthians 4:4, "In whom the god of this world hath blinded the minds of them which believe not, lest the light of the glorious gospel of Christ, who is the image of God, should shine unto them."

3. Man is spiritually deaf. Acts 7:57, "Then they cried out with a loud voice, and stopped their ears, and ran upon him with one accord."

4. Romans 3:10–18 is a death knell. "As it is written, There is none righteous, no, not one: There is none that understandeth, there is none that seeketh after God. They are all gone out of the way, they are together become unprofitable; there is none that doeth good, no, not one. Their throat is an open sepulchre; with their tongues they have used deceit; the poison of asps is under their lips: whose mouth is full of cursing and bitterness: their feet are swift to shed blood: destruction and misery are in their ways: and the way of peace have they not known: there is no fear of God before their eyes."

The lost man can't do anything good. He can't see right, speak right, think right, or live right. According to Romans 3, the lost man is hopelessly lost and needs someone to lead him to Christ.

The Bible says come out, and the New Evangelical says stay in. The New Evangelical says infiltrate, but the Bible says separate. The New Evangelical says he's tired of fighting, but Paul was still fighting in II Timothy 4:7: "I have fought a good fight, I have finished my course, I have kept the faith."

It seems that the position of New Evangelicals is that the ends justify the means. New Evangelicals seem to succeed in many of their goals. Their influence is worldwide, but so is that of the Charismatics and cults. Bless your soul, so are the Fundamentalists, and as long as God lends us breath, we will stand for Christ and everything that pleases Him.

We take the philosophy of Nehemiah 4:17: "They which builded on the wall, and they that bare burdens, with those that laded, every one with one of his hands wrought in the work, and with the other hand held a weapon." The prophet's job was to rebuild the wall. He had many enemies outside the wall and inside the wall. His challenge was to build the wall and to defend it from his enemies. Verse 17 gives us God's solution "Every one with one of his hands wrought in the work, and with the other hand held a weapon." One hand to rebuild, and the other to defend. I believe this is the true picture of real Fundamentalism.

In 1956, men began to teach this New Evangelicalism and to some degree it looked successful. They wrote many books and many articles, but the plan had one very large hitch. Getting it into the churches and graduate schools was easy, but getting it into the pews was the hitch. The pews were filled with old-time Methodists, Bible-reading Presbyterians, even some Lutherans, and Episcopalians, and last but not least those Baptists. The problem remained how to get those Bible believers in the pew to swallow this new hunk of baloney.

Then it happened. Out of the blue came America's newest evangelist, who burst on the scene. After several crusades, Dr. Harold Ockenga and others persuaded Dr. William Graham to incorporate under the name of "The Billy Graham Evangelistic Association." Dr. Graham did not stop their policies, and procedures were changed. His demand was that churches who cooperated must be willing to make it a fifty-fifty proposition, one half evangelical and the other half liberal and modernists. The cry-word was "anything for souls." America's Fundamentalists had never seen football stadiums filled and hundreds and thousands coming forward for salvation.

So many fundamental churches split. Pastors lost their churches. The cry-word from the pew was that if people didn't cooperate, they were against souls getting saved.

Another new policy was that all churches that cooperated would get converts sent back to their churches. Many priests and those in authority recommended liberal churches, which consisted of modernistic Methodists, Roman Catholics, and so forth. I went to the Methodist church in Lansdale to talk to the pastor. I asked him if he believed in the literal, physical resurrection of Jesus Christ from the dead. His answer was "No, certainly not; no intelligent person believes that anymore." This pastor was *the county chairman of Lansdale's crusade.*

THE BATTLE AGAINST NEW EVANGELICALISM

Another example is from the "Blue Print," in a letter dated March 19, 1965, to a gentleman in North Carolina, the Reverend Cuthert E. Allen of the Catholic Belmont Abbey College. He wrote as follows, "Billy Graham gave an inspiring and theologically sound address that may have been given by Bishop Fulton J. Sheen or any other Catholic preacher. I have followed Billy Graham's career, and I must emphasize that he had been more Catholic than otherwise."

Please tell me how a dead man can cooperate in the salvation of dead men. Both Christ and Paul are our New Testament examples with Nehemiah of the Old Testament. Both the Old Testament and the New Testament tell us that unbelievers have no part in the work of God. Our debt to the lost is not cooperation, but separation. Nehemiah's plan was simple when the heathen wanted to cooperate; Nehemiah 2:20 says, "Then answered I them, and said unto them, the God of heaven, he will prosper us; therefore we his servants will arise and build: but ye have no portion, nor right, nor memorial, in Jerusalem." Second Chronicles 19:1–2 says, "And Jehoshaphat the king of Judah returned to his house in peace to Jerusalem. And Jehu the son of Hanani the seer went out to meet him, and said to king Jehoshaphat, Shouldest thou help the ungodly, and love them that hate the Lord? therefore is wrath upon thee from before the Lord." Ezra 4:1–3 says, "Now when the adversaries of Judah and Benjamin heard that the children of the captivity builded the temple unto the Lord God of Israel; then they came to Zerubbabel, and to the chief of the fathers, and said unto them, Let us build with you: for we seek your God, as ye do; and we do sacrifice unto him since the days of Esar-haddon king of Assur, which brought us up hither. But Zerubbabel, and Jeshua, and the rest of the chief of the fathers of Israel, said unto them, Ye have nothing to do with us to build an house unto our God; but we ourselves together will build unto the Lord God of Israel, as king Cyrus the king of Persia hath commanded us."

I have fought New Evangelicalism for over fifty years with no regrets because it is such a destructive movement. I've lost many friends, but the truth is more important than friendship. We've lost church members over it, but many have written or returned, realizing that we were biblical. Many pastors and church members have shipwrecked over it. Therefore, we do not apologize for standing against New Evangelicals.

God have mercy on believing pastors and other believers who have plunged into this philosophy of keeping up with the crowd, keeping peace in the church and home. We should not cooperate with evil. The Fundamentalist cry-words are separation, noncooperation, preach the Bible at all cost, and preach the whole counsel of God. Let God be the judge. You have two choices.

I included this chapter in my book because of a study I did of the book of Acts and the Epistles to see if Paul infiltrated. Did Paul get recognition from the Jews or Rome? Did Paul seek their praise? *Of course, the answer is an emphatic NO.*

Second Corinthians 11:23–28 says

> Are they ministers of Christ? (I speak as a fool) I am more; in labours more abundant, in stripes above measure, in prisons more frequent, in deaths oft. Of the Jews five times received I forty stripes save one. Thrice was I beaten with rods, once was I stoned, thrice I suffered shipwreck, a night and a day I have been in the deep; in journeyings often, in perils of waters, in perils of robbers, in perils by mine own countrymen, in perils by the heathen, in perils in the city, in perils in the wilderness, in perils in the sea, in perils among false brethren; in weariness and painfulness, in watchings often, in hunger and thirst, in fastings often, in cold and nakedness. Beside those things that are without, that which cometh upon me daily, *the care of all the churches.*

In these few verses Paul gives a trial of sorrow, pain, suffering, and heartache. His description of his life would shame the angels. At no time did he seek comfort of the lost. Listen to how he describes his life. He shows at least twenty-seven pains and perils in his life.

Ephesians 2:12 says, "That at that time ye were without Christ, being aliens from the commonwealth of Israel, and strangers from the covenants of promise, having no hope, and without God in the world." How can we get together with unbelievers and do God's will? It is impossible, and it is sin when men try.

The New Evangelical is smug in his comfort and proud of how much freedom he has by not being bound by God's rules and standards. He even claims that the majority is on his side. It reminds me of one who bragged about being free from laws, rules, and commands. He was told that a train is only free when it is on the track. When it gets free from the track, it goes nowhere. As a matter of fact, as soon as it is free from the track, it is wrecked.

THE BATTLE
AGAINST CALVINISM

At the recommendation of my pastor, I applied to the Reformed Episcopal Seminary and was accepted. I was not prepared for my first day in class. The professor prayed and then said, "Gentlemen, I will be your teacher of theology for the next three years. Know this, first, last, and always; God is the author of sin."

I raised my hand and asked him to repeat that and say it slowly, which he did. When the initial shock wore off, I was on my feet objecting to this heresy. For three years he taught it, and for three years I objected loud and long.

There are three main theologies: Calvinism, Arminianism, Biblicist.

For the lack of a better name, I accept the last one. The Calvinist says you must be a Calvinist or an Arminian. So my professors and other students called me a Calmenian. I didn't care as long as they didn't call me a Calvinist.

- Calvinist—One who accepts John Calvin's theory of sovereignty and his doctrine of TULIP.
- Arminian—One who accepts Jacob Arminius's doctrine of limited salvation. He taught that a believer could sin so severely that he could forfeit his salvation.

- Biblicist—One who makes the Bible the sole rule of faith and practice.

I believe most of the men in my class believed as I did, but by the end of the first year the vast majority were full-fledged Calvinists. And what's even sadder is that many who call themselves fundamental Baptists are in fact secret Calvinists. They are afraid to come out and say so. They save their Calvinism for their study and feed their congregation Calvinism in small doses. Our seminary, Calvary Baptist Theological Seminary, is one of the few seminaries that take a stand against Calvinism. I had a professor who said in the pulpit, "I am an *Arminian,*" and in the classroom, "I am a *Calvinist.*" Many of these secret Calvinists cover by saying, "I'm only a two pointer or a three pointer." I want the world to know that I am a *no pointer.*

CALVINISM

- Supralapsarian—God predestinates to heaven and hell. He chooses every action also.
- Infralapsarian—God predestinates only to heaven.

(If all men are dead and can't save themselves, and God is almighty and can save them all but chooses to save a few, then in fact He sends men to hell.)

Some Calvinists believe that God predestinates all words and actions. Some believe that He only predestinates some. But there is no agreement among them.

Some familiar words in Calvinism

- Foreknowledge—To know ahead
- Predestination—To determine ahead
- Chosen—To select or appoint
- Election—To choose out; sovereignty; absolute

A LOOK AT CALVIN'S DOCTRINE

T—Total Depravity. All men are spiritually dead. Dead men can do nothing and can never please God. Man thinks wrong, lives wrong, and is totally wrong.

- Jeremiah 17:9—"The heart is deceitful above all things, and desperately wicked: who can know it?"
- Ephesians 2:1—"And you hath He quickened, who were dead in trespasses and sins."
- Psalm 58:3—"The wicked are estranged from the womb: they go astray as soon as they be born, speaking lies."
- Romans 3:10–12—"As it is written, There is none righteous, no, not one: there is none that understandeth, there is none that seeketh after God. They are all gone out of the way, they are together become unprofitable; there is none that doeth good, no, not one."

My answer to "T" is that there is no doubt that fundamental Baptists believe this, too, but with one great exception. Calvinists believe that God Almighty made man to fall into sin, while fundamental Baptists believe that all men are born that way. There is a great difference between creating man and his becoming depraved and his being born that way.

U—Unconditional Election. There are no conditions that man must meet in order for God to save him. Calvinists use John 15:16: "Ye have not chosen me, but I have chosen you, and ordained you, that ye should go and bring forth fruit, and that your fruit should remain: that whatsoever ye shall ask of the Father in my name, he may give it you."

My answer to "U" is John 3:16. "For God so loved the world, that he gave his *only begotten son, that whosoever believeth* in him should not perish, but have everlasting life." This verse certainly denies unconditional election. It says that man must believe.

Hebrews 11:6 says *you must believe.* "But without faith it is impossible to please him: for he that cometh to God must believe that he is, and that he is a rewarder of them that diligently seek him."

Romans 10:13 says that *man must call.* "For whosoever shall call upon the name of the Lord shall be saved."

John 1:12 says that *man must receive* Christ. "But as many as received him, to them gave he power to become the sons of God, even to them that believe on his name."

Luke 13:3–5 says that *man must repent.* "I tell you, Nay: but, except ye repent, ye shall all likewise perish. Or those eighteen, upon whom the tower in Siloam fell, and slew them, think ye that they were sinners above all men that dwelt in Jerusalem? I tell you, Nay: but, except ye repent, ye shall all likewise perish."

L—Limited Atonement. This means that Christ's death was not for everyone, but only for those that His Father predestinated.

My answer to "L" is that it is sad when a pastor gets so hard up for a proof text that he destroys the Word of God. Listen to the Calvinists' text in Matthew 1:21: "And she shall bring forth a son, and thou shalt call his name JESUS: for he shall save his people from their sins." Does that mean His people or the Calvinists are the only elect? The precious blood of Christ should not be wasted on sinners that God did not intend to save.

Acts 20:28 says, "Take heed therefore unto yourselves, and to all the flock, over the which the Holy Ghost hath made you overseers, to feed the church of God, which he hath purchased with his own blood." Again the Calvinist says that the *church of God* means the elected; the predestinated were purchased with His blood. *I call this blasphemy!* I do not believe a believer can go any lower than to deny the death of our Lord to all sinners.

I—Irresistible Grace. The Calvinists mean by this that if a person has been chosen to salvation, then he must believe that there will come a time, a place, and a date when the Spirit will come upon him, and he cannot resist Him. He must get saved. If God has chosen someone, He will give him a desire to come.

John 10:26 says, "But ye believe not, because ye are not of my sheep, as I said unto you."

My answer to "I" is that this could be said to any crowd in the world. There is nothing in this passage about resisting. What does Scripture say? In Acts 7:51, Stephen addresses the high priest and says, "Ye stiffnecked and uncircumcised in heart and ears, ye do always *resist the Holy Ghost:* as your fathers did, so do ye."

Second Timothy 3:8 says, "Now as Jannes and Jambres withstood Moses, so do these also *resist the truth*: men of corrupt minds, reprobate concerning the faith."

Matthew 23:37 says, "O Jerusalem, Jerusalem, thou that killest the prophets, and stonest them which are sent unto thee, how often would I have gathered thy children together, even as a hen gathereth her chickens under her wings, and *ye would not*!"

Notice what our Lord says to the lost Pharisees and Sadducees. He did not say *ye could not*, nor did He say *ye did not*. But He did say *ye would not*, showing that by the act of their own will they would not come.

P—Perseverance of the Saints. By this the Calvinist means that those who are chosen and predestinated will persevere unto the end and not fall away. One of their texts, Matthew 24, is primarily to the Jewish nation, not the church age.

I reject "P" because to the Calvinist his salvation must be future. It can't be now because he can know that he is saved only as long as he is persevering. He ends up in the same boiling pot as the Arminian. That is why I said before that I am a *no pointer.* fundamental Baptists do great harm when they say they are a two pointer or a three pointer. *All five points are man-made.*

After all of these years, it is time to throw off the bondage of this man-made system. We should be fundamental Baptists and *not Protestants.*

THE CALVINIST'S DILEMMA

Whosoever? This can't be true, so a Calvinist adds words like "whosoever of the elect" in John 3:16. It should read, "For God so loved the world that he gave his only begotten son that *whosoever of the elect* that believeth in him should not perish, but have everlasting life." It's too bad the Holy Spirit didn't think of that when He inspired holy men of God to write the Scriptures.

A free gift, found in Romans 5:18. "Therefore as by the offence of one judgment came upon all men to condemnation; even so by the righteousness of one the free gift came upon all men unto justification of life."

The word of *God* from the Bible. God wants all to be saved. In I Timothy 2:4 we read, "Who will have all men to be saved, and to come unto the knowledge of the truth." He intends to have mercy upon all. Romans 11:32 says, "For God hath concluded them all in unbelief, that he might have mercy upon all." Jesus Christ is the ransom for all. First Timothy 2:6 says, "Who gave himself a ransom for all, to be testified in due time."

THE EFFECT OF CALVINISM ON
OTHER DOCTRINES IN THE BIBLE

The doctrine of prayer. If God has ordained everything, why pray? Prayer will not change God or anything else. The Calvinist, because of his doctrine, can't believe prayer will change things. The Calvinist prays because he is ordained to pray. He never prays because God is the source of his needs. In Joshua 10:12 we read, "Then spake Joshua to the Lord in the day when the Lord delivered up the Amorites before the children of Israel, and he said in the sight of Israel, Sun, stand thou still upon Gibeon; and thou, Moon, in the valley of Ajalon." Joshua prayed that God would stop the sun from going down so that he could have a longer day to finish the battle. And God did it! "Ye have not, because ye ask not." But a Calvinist would read it, *"Ye have not because I ordained not."* James 4:2 says, "Ye lust, and have not: ye kill, and desire to have, and cannot obtain: ye fight and war, yet ye have not, because ye ask not."

Moses was God's leader during the Exodus. Moses prayed for meat and it came; he prayed for water and it came. *Yes, prayer changes things.*

The doctrine of rewards. You wicked and shameful servant.

- I ordained you to build with hay, wood, and stubble.
- I ordained that you be unforgiving.
- I ordained that you be carnal and lazy.

- I ordained that you be backslidden.
- I ordained that you be a gossiper and a backbiter.

Therefore you will lose your reward! Ezekiel 3:18 says, "When I say unto the wicked, Thou shalt surely die; and thou givest him not warning, nor speakest to warn the wicked from his wicked way, to save his life; the same wicked man shall die in his iniquity; but his blood will I require at thine hand." Ezekiel 33:6 says, "But if the watchman see the sword come, and blow not the trumpet, and the people be not warned; if the sword come, and take any person from among them, he is taken away in his iniquity; but his blood will I require at the watchman's hand."

The words *reward, rewarder, rewardeth* are mentioned over one hundred times in the Bible. The word simply means that which is given in return for good or evil.

Can you ever imagine a scene like this? Two dedicated Calvinists stand before the judgment seat of Christ, and the Lord says to the one on the right,

"Calvinist, well done, good Calvinist. I made you generous and you were ordained to be faithful. I also ordained that you would be kind and compassionate. You certainly were great and did all that I ordained you to be. Because you were obedient to my commands, I am going to reward you."

Then He says to the Calvinist on the left, "Since you did everything I ordained you to do—lie, cheat, steal—I must ordain you to lose your reward."

The doctrine of morality. Many of my classmates at Reformed Episcopal Seminary smoked and drank around the seminary for years. They reasoned, "Why not; what's going to be is going to be, and you can't resist it." There is no real place for the fear of God in the Calvinist system, *because the fear of God is to depart from evil!*

Loraine Boettner in his book entitled *The Reformed Doctrine of Predestination* writes on page 239, "All evil forces are under absolute control and could be blotted out of existence in an instant *if He willed. The murderer is kept in life and is indebted to God for the strength to kill his victim,* and also for the opportunity." His biblical proofs are Job 12:16: "With him is strength and wisdom: the deceived and the deceiver are his." *Wow! Boettner says every sin is ordained!*

The doctrine of soulwinning. I had a Calvinist tell me the reason for soulwinning is that we do not know just who is elected, so we must go. I said to him, "Do you mean that God gives you a choice of going or not? If He does, you make Him contradict Himself. Why not wait around until He ordains you to go?" The man had no answer for me.

Fundamental Baptist theology is not based on the views of a man, but on a complete study of the *Word of God.*

The Protestant, or Calvinist theology, is the same and is built on *man's interpretation, not God's Word. In the case of Calvinist theology, it was built on one key man, Calvin, not the Word of God.* The Biblicist, or fundamental Baptist, builds all theology on the Word of God. For Calvinism to make some sense, Calvinists must keep adding, subtracting, or changing definitions. Because of this, they have many problem passages. *They change "world" to "the world of the elect," "all" to "all of the elect," and "whosoever" to "whosoever of the elect."*

According to the Bible, God does predestinate. The difference between a Calvinist and a Biblicist is not the *doctrine* of predestination, but *when* God predestinates and *how* He did it? Does the Bible give to us a clear-cut answer? *Yes! Yes! Yes!*

Let's look at two passages. Romans 8:29 does not change it. Do not reinterpret it; just read what it does say. "For whom he did *foreknow*, he also did predestinate." He chose and predestinated based on what He knew man would do when man heard.

First Peter 1:2 says, "Elect according to the *foreknowledge* of God." Notice it does not say "elect according to the sovereignty of God." That is what the Calvinists say. So we have found the answer to the first question—God predestinates based on His foreknowledge.

Question two, when does God predestinate? The answer is clear; He predestinated before the foundation of the world. Ephesians 1:4 says, "According as he hath chosen us in him before the foundation of the world, that we should be holy and without blame before him in love." The Calvinist will come with this charge: God is sovereign; He is omnipresent and omnipotent. If He permits man to make a choice, He loses His sovereignty. Calvinists have to stand on their heads to prove that charge. Biblicists agree that God is sovereign. We also agree that man is born dead in trespasses and sin. But God's plans are perfect. Please follow me through the Bible.

Before the world was, God ordained a perfect plan for man. He would have creatures for His needs and brethren with whom He could fellowship. Hebrews 2:10 says, "For it became him, for whom are all things, and by whom are all things, in bringing many sons unto glory, to make the captain of their salvation perfect through sufferings." God knows all things, and man's rebellion was not a surprise to Him. The Calvinist says that God ordained Adam to sin. The image of God in man included several things including a *will* to choose. God permitted man to make that choice, but to say that God ordained him to sin is nonsense.

God's plan can't be corrupted because God's plan included a Savior who by His birth and sinless life, His death, resurrection, and soon coming again *made God's plan perfect and made a way of salvation for fallen man.*

God created

Man—"So God created man in his own image, in the image of God created he him; male and female created he them" (Gen. 1:27).

Hell—"Then shall he say also unto them on the left hand, Depart from me, ye cursed, into everlasting fire, prepared for the devil and his angels" (Matt. 25:41).

No surprise to God

God's plan

Before the foundation of the world

A Savior

Man is dead and can't help

God's plan was to give fallen man *two gifts:*

Light to see. John 1:9—"That was the true Light, which lighteth every man that cometh into the world." Man is blind, but God gives him light so that as a blind man he can see when the gospel is brought to him.

Enabling grace so all can respond. Titus 2:11—"For the grace of God that bringeth salvation hath appeared to all men." Notice, *it doesn't say* that salvation has appeared to all men, *but the grace that bringeth salvation has appeared to all men. This allows the lost man to have the God-given ability to receive the gospel and be saved.*

THE BATTLE

AGAINST THE FLESH

Shortly after my salvation, I realized that something was wrong. Almost no one was glad that I was no longer a drunk, a cusser, a brawler, a gambler, or a general bum. My brother and sisters disowned me. My old drinking buddies suddenly disowned me. Most of my old drinking buddies disappeared, and those that stayed took great delight in mocking me, especially if there was a crowd around. I thought that getting saved settled all problems. I was in for a shock! When you are in military service, you are under the microscope twenty-four hours a day. You eat, sleep, and work with the lost. Once you declare yourself to be saved, they watch your every move. They get to see many hypocrites, and they will be glad when you fall.

I began to watch three people—the Lord Jesus Christ, the apostle Paul, and myself. I never saw much joy or happiness in the Lord's life. What joy I did see was in living for us, suffering for us, and dying for us. His single joy is found in Matthew 25:21: "His Lord said unto him, Well done, thou good and faithful servant: thou hast been faithful over a few things, I will make thee ruler over many things; enter thou into the *joy* of thy lord." In Hebrews 12:2 we read, "Looking unto Jesus the author and finisher of our faith; who for the *joy* that was set before him endured the cross, despising the shame, and is set down at the right hand of the throne of God." John 15:20 says, "Remember the word that I said unto you, The servant is not greater than his lord. If they have persecuted me, they will also persecute you; if they have kept my saying, they will keep yours also."

If the world sees Christ in me, it should treat me as Christ was treated. He had many battles, so I should have many battles.

Paul, the great apostle, is another example of a life filled with battles. He wrote in II Corinthians 11:23–28,

> Are they ministers of Christ? (I speak as a fool) I am more; in labours more abundant, in stripes above measure, in prisons more frequent, in deaths oft. Of the Jews five times received I forty stripes save one. Thrice was I beaten with rods, once was I stoned, thrice I suffered shipwreck, a night and a day I have been in the deep; in journeyings often, in perils of water, in perils of robbers, in perils by mine own countrymen, in perils by the heathen, in perils in the city, in perils in the wilderness, in perils in the sea, in perils among false brethren; in weariness and painfulness, in watchings often, in hunger and thirst, in fastings often, in cold and nakedness. Beside those things that are without, that which cometh upon me daily, the care of all the churches.

As Paul described his battles, it sounds as though Satan had turned the hordes of hell against him. Yet Paul didn't think it wrong that he should be treated like Christ. It is true that our Lord and Paul as well as Peter and the others apostles had a lifetime of battles. First Peter 4:12–13 states, "Beloved, think it not strange concerning the fiery trial which is to try you, as though some strange thing happened unto you: but rejoice, inasmuch as ye are partakers of Christ's sufferings; that, when his glory shall be revealed, ye may be glad also with exceeding joy."

The believer's life is filled with *joy, peace, blessings, and fulfillment. However,* you can expect that if the life you choose is lived biblically you will be continually facing the battlefield. Our Lord expects us to attack with the power of the Holy Spirit to *win.* I asked my pastor one day, "Will there come a time in my lifetime when the battles will stop?" His answer was yes, when you die or when our

Lord returns, and there is one thing you can be sure of, *it will be one day*!

This battle against the flesh is by far the *hardest battle I have fought*. Only death or the Rapture will stop it. It starts the moment you are saved and ends only at death or the coming of Christ. When God created man, He made him in His own image. God is a Spirit, so God made Adam a spirit being robed in flesh. Genesis 1:27 says, "So God created man in his own image, in the image of God created he him; male and female created he them."

God also made man with a will to choose *right* from *wrong*. We read in Genesis 2:16–17, "And the Lord God commanded the man, saying, Of every tree of the garden thou mayest freely eat: but of the tree of the knowledge of good and evil, *thou shalt not eat of it:* for in the day that thou eatest thereof thou shalt surely die." God also placed before Adam a test and a penalty.

Adam fell into sin and God carried out the penalty: "Thou shalt surely die." Adam died spiritually; he actually lived nine hundred thirty years. *What happened?* Remember that God had created Adam as a physical man and a spiritual man. Adam did not immediately die physically, but he died spiritually. He was now a spiritually *dead* man. He needed to be born again. He was now a fallen creature and could no longer walk with God. In John 4:23–24 we read, "But the hour cometh, and now is, when the true worshippers shall worship the Father in spirit and in truth: for the Father seeketh such to worship him. God is a Spirit: and they that worship him must worship him in spirit and in truth."

You can imagine my surprise to learn that there was a reason for the new birth. An even greater surprise was to find that God would hold me responsible for my life from the new birth to death. *However*, being a great and loving God, He would supply all that I needed to live that life.

- II Corinthians 5:10—"For we must all appear before the judgment seat of Christ; that every one may receive the things done in his body, according to that he hath done, whether it be good or bad."

- Romans 14:12—"So then every one of us shall give account of himself to God."

One reason that I believe so highly in discipleship courses is that the new believer is responsible for his every word, thought, and deed. One of the saddest things I know is that an evangelical church or soulwinner will lead a soul to Christ and not do a follow-up on that new believer. That church and soulwinner are living in disobedience and cause the new believer to sin, unless they can say to God, "Lord, *I commit him to You because I can't do it.*"

I hadn't been saved for more than a few days and out of my mouth came a string of cuss words. Right away I felt like a traitor and was ashamed. I felt ashamed because I had told all seventy-two sailors in my division that I had gotten saved. I had been warned that they would be watching, and they watched me day and night. When those words came out, they laughed, mocked, and screamed. It only took about ten minutes for the whole ship to know about my slip of the tongue. I was about two weeks old in the Lord, and I had thought that salvation took care of all those things.

I learned that there was a piece missing in my conversion and that was to grow in grace and in knowledge. But you can't do that in two weeks, and I was impatient to gain knowledge. I soon found out that I had at least one advantage. Because I was in the United States Navy, when we left port, I had a lot more time to read my Bible. I found that if I used just the time that I wasted, I could read the whole Bible through six times a year. *Now, if you do not believe that statement*, try it and don't cheat. Ephesians 5:16 says, "Redeeming the time, because the days are evil." Count the time you are going anywhere by car. You can buy the Bible on cassette and listen and drive at the same time. You will be amazed at the results. Count the many times you have waited around just picking up your children. Count the time watching television. Count the useless chatter on the phone. Count also the endless nights you can't sleep. Don't count sheep. Get up and read your Bible. It is amazing that we can find time for a hundred other things, but it is so hard to find the time to feed our souls. Is it any wonder that there is no revival? Is it any wonder that it takes a war or a death to get us in our Bibles? Is it any wonder that divorce is running at a record pace among believers? Amos 8:11 says, "Behold, the days come, saith the Lord God, that I will send a famine in the land, not a famine of bread, nor a thirst for water, but of hearing the words of the Lord." The sad truth is that in many believers' lives the only Bible they get is the verses they hear read in church on Sunday.

Dear believer, the bride of Christ could use a real hot sin-destroying revival because you and I both know that the church has been in hibernation a very long time.

Hundreds of times believers have come to me as their pastor and all of them sound the same. "Pastor, I hate the ups and downs of believers. Is there not some simple study, some key passages that would simplify a study? And then I could read them and study them and could, by the grace of God, bring consistency to my walk with the Lord." This troubled me, and after several months of praying and *fasting,* I finally had peace about giving this Bible study to our whole church. I believed from the beginning that there was some kind of key that would accomplish this goal. I prayed to the Lord that He would direct my mind so that when I was ready to give the study to the church it truly would be biblical and simple. *It dawned on me after I had studied that God meant it for me, too!*

I studied and a single word kept coming to my mind. It was the word *daily.* The church responded very well. I took the outline and put it on a small card that was sticky on one side and had the daily study on the other side.

Most believers are lazy, and like our generation, we want everything short, easy, and with no sweat. If I were to say to you, I have found the *key* to the greatest medicine that cures all diseases, and I could prove it to you that you could stay healthy and well until you were old and died, would you believe it? If I said that you could live completely well if you went to the doctor's office every day, all day for a whole year, would you believe it? *No one could stop you from believing and doing it, because you want to be well!*

If I came to your church and said, "Folks, I have found the *key* to financial success and becoming a millionaire, and all you have to do is read the Constitution and Bill of Rights of the United States in one sitting." *There would be no stopping you because we all want to be more financially secure.*

If I came to your church and said, "Folks, I have found in God's Word how to become a truly spiritual person with the power to be pleasing to the Lord. But you must do eight things a day, every day. How many would come?" You know this announcement would not cause a great commotion, *for just a few believers want to be spiritual. They really do not want all the world to be spiritual.*

To become a victorious believer is not a gift *but a reward.* The *key* to joyful obedience and the *key* to having a life pleasing to the Lord is never forgetting that we will always have three enemies— the *world,* the *flesh,* and the *Devil.* None of these three will ever be your friend. That's why we need a daily walk with God and daily food from God's Word.

THE KEY

The question that has been most asked of me and hundreds of other pastors and Christian workers is "Pastor, how can I live the Christian life successfully? What is the key to getting 'up' for the Lord and staying up for Christ, not being up and down, and off and on, hot and cold, not backsliding, and becoming cold and indifferent, and proud of the few verses of Scripture that I know? How can I know joy, real joy, wonderful joy, all the days of my Christian life? Is it possible?"

The Goal of God for the Christian

1. II Corinthians 2:14—"Now thanks be unto God, which always causeth us to triumph in Christ." We do not always triumph, do we?

2. Romans 8:38–39—"For I am persuaded, that neither death, nor life, nor angels, nor principalities, nor powers, nor things present, nor things to come, nor height, nor depth, nor any other creature, shall be able to separate us from the love of God

which is in Christ Jesus our Lord." We allow a lot of things to separate us from the love of God.

3. Galatians 2:20—"I am crucified with Christ: nevertheless I live; yet not I, but Christ liveth in me: and the life which I now live in the flesh I live by the faith of the Son of God, who loved me, and gave himself for me." We are not always crucified.

4. I Corinthians 15:57—"But thanks be to God, which giveth us the victory through our Lord Jesus Christ." There are many thousands of Christians who are defeated.

5. I Peter 1:8—"Whom having not seen, ye love; in whom, though now ye see him not, yet believing, ye rejoice with joy unspeakable and full of glory." A lot of Christians don't have joy unspeakable and full of glory.

6. II Corinthians 13:11—"Finally, brethren, farewell. Be perfect, be of good comfort, be of one mind, live in peace; and the God of love and peace shall be with you." Christians don't have peace. They don't live together in harmony. There is turmoil and division on every hand.

7. Galatians 1:4—"Who gave himself for our sins, that he might deliver us from this present evil world, according to the will of God and our Father." There are millions of Christians who are not delivered from this present evil age.

And so we have a difference between our walk and our state, a difference between what we have been promised and what we have claimed. We have a difference between what we call the ideal and the practical. It seems, at least to the average Christian, that all the promises of God are in the future, and none are for him right now. Many of God's children turn back and walk no more with Him because they try to live the Christian life, and they get so completely discouraged trying to live it that they finally say, "It can't be lived." They believe that those promises of "always causing us to triumph," promises of always giving us the victory, those promises of "joy unspeakable and full of glory" can't be now, but are for the future. They couldn't be for now because no one can live a Christian life without falling, without being up and down, without backsliding.

Yet, dear child of God, we read in II Peter 1:10, "If ye do these things, ye shall *never fall*." *It is possible* to be a Christian every day of your Christian life, to continue growing in your knowledge, love, joy, and virtuous life. *It is possible* to be a Christian and every day of your Christian life be filled with the Spirit of God. *It is possible* to be a Christian and have joy and victory and triumph in Christ day in and day out. *It is possible* to be a Christian and be a daily, weekly soulwinner for the Lord Jesus Christ without allowing depression, defeat, and the pull of this world to take you down and make you like you were before you were saved.

I say to you that *it is possible* because the Bible says, "If you *do these things,* you will *never* fall." I want to give you eight steps to success. The very first thing you have to do before you do any of these is to give your life to Christ. You have to surrender yourself to the Lord. Unless you are a dedicated Christian, these things done daily won't work in your life. If you have sin in your life, you are away from Christ. To have a dedicated Christian life, you must give your life totally, completely, unconditionally back to Jesus Christ. Surrender everything that you have and are to Him. Once you do that, you can do these daily things. But don't try to do these things and think you will have a Christian life on top of your old sin. You must repent of your sin, come back to Jesus Christ, and surrender your life to Him.

All eight things begin with the same word. To be successful in the Lord Jesus Christ and in the Christian life, you only have to remember to practice one word in your life. That word is not the *Lord Jesus Christ,* although the name of the Lord is the name that is above every name. That word is not the word *Love,* though love expresses all that God has for us and wants us to be. That word is not the *Second Coming* of Jesus Christ, although that is the best hope of every child of God. There is one word, and if every child of God will pray and put that word upon his or her heart so that he or she never forgets it, that person will always have a dedicated, victorious, soulwinning, Spirit-filled, Christian life. A word that is so mundane that when you hear it, you are always disappointed. Yet with this word athletes break all the records in the world; with this word inventors have given us light; with this word, men have changed the world and made it livable for us. What is the word? *Daily.*

If you will do eight things daily in your life, Monday through Monday, January through January, year one of your saved life until you die, you will be able to say, "By the grace of God, I have never backslidden. By the grace of God I have had a growing, glowing, sowing, and reaping Christian life." Take the eight times in which the Word of God says *daily* and ask the Spirit of God to brand it upon your mind so that you think about it the first thing every morning. If you will do these things every single day of your life, you will never fall. The athlete who goes to the Olympics runs every day. The man who won the mile in the Olympics ran thirty miles every day—that's why he won. Anything you do in life, you do it every day and you will become good at it.

Not eating every day has an effect upon you. You eat daily to make you healthy. Why is heart disease taking thousands upon thousands out of this life? They don't exercise. Many people want to go out and run twenty miles once a year. They drop dead. You must do it every day to have a healthy body. You know very well that kids would like to go to school every third Monday of every other week. To them school becomes monotonous and boring. They need to go every day to get an education. Work daily and you will have food and security. Why are Christians defeated? Because Christians are lazy; they don't want to be successful.

Even if you don't know how to button your shirt, if you do these eight things every day God promises you holiness, godliness, fruitfulness, and fullness of the Spirit. You will have all of these things if you get out of bed every morning and do eight things for God.

Die—Daily

You have to die every day. We read in I Corinthians 15:31 that Paul said, "I die daily." He further explains in II Corinthians 4:10, "Always bearing about in the body the dying of the Lord Jesus, that the life also of Jesus might be made manifest in our body." The first mistake a Christian makes is getting up in the morning and going to work without praying. The minute you get out of bed you should get down on your knees and say, "Lord, I want You to take my life today. I want You to let me die to sin and be alive to Christ. I want my life dead to every single thing today that You are against." Paul said, "I die daily." You *die* that He might live in you. The trouble is that morning after morning after morning you get up and live instead of letting Jesus Christ live in your body. "The life which I now live in the flesh I live by the faith of the Son of God, who loved me, and gave himself for me" (Gal. 2:20). We must pray, Take my life and let it be, consecrated, Lord, to Thee. Take my lips and let them speak. Take my ears and let them hear. Take my feet and let them move. Take my hands." You die and let Him live in your life.

Read the Word of God—Daily

We read in the book of Acts that when the apostle Paul had gone from Thessalonica to Berea he said, "These were more noble than those in Thessalonica, in that they received the word with all readiness of mind, and searched the Scriptures daily, whether those things were so." I want you to see that it is the positive that God puts here, not the negative. These Christians did not go to the Bible to find out if Paul was wrong; they received the Word with gladness of heart and they daily searched the Scripture to affirm that what Paul said was absolutely true.

In Isaiah 34:16 we read, "Seek ye out of the book of the Lord, and read: no one of these shall fail, none shall want her mate: for my mouth it hath commanded, and his Spirit it hath gathered them." Psalm 1 says, "Blessed is the man that walketh not in the counsel of the ungodly, nor standeth in the way of sinners, nor sitteth in the seat of the scornful. But his delight is in the law of the Lord; and in his law doth he meditate day and night." We should first of all pray before we read the Bible, asking the Lord to make us see something out of His Word today and give us a blessing. Then read the Word of God. How do you read it? Your reading must be systematic. In other words, start at one of the books in the Bible, such as the Gospel of John, read a couple of chapters a day until you finish John. After that book go to the books of Acts, Romans, I and II Corinthians, and continue until you have finished the entire Bible. When you have read it all, start all over again. Why? The Bible says, "Thy word have I hid in mine heart, that I might not sin against thee" (Ps. 119:11). Don't backslide. I guarantee you that the vast majority of Christians do not daily read the Word of God, and then they wonder why they can't have a successful Christian life. People come down the aisle and say, "I want to read my Bible, and I want to start praying." *You must repent first of all, turn from all your old evil ways and all of your old evil friends as a Christian, and come clean for Christ.* Once you come clean for Him, you must die every day. Second of all, you must read the Word of God every day. Every single day you must eat the Word of God. Jeremiah says, "Thy words were found and I did eat them, and they were to me the joy and rejoicing of my soul, for I am called by thy name, O Lord God of Hosts."

Take Up Your Cross—Daily

Luke 9:23 says, "If any man will come after me, let him deny himself, and take up his cross daily, and follow me." What does it mean to take up your cross daily? The last words tell us what it means: it means to follow Jesus Christ. Whatever He wants me to do every single day is what I will do. I'm not quiet when I should be speaking; I'm not speaking when I should be silent. I present the crucified Christ to every single person that God gives me the opportunity to tell. I take up my cross and follow Him every single day. The Bible says, "He that followeth me shall not walk in darkness, but he shall have the light of life" (John 8:12).

No Christian that follows Christ will walk into a barroom or a race track or a girlie magazine place. No Christian that is following Jesus will gossip on the telephone, have hate or incest in his heart, or lust because he is following the Lord daily.

That means that every day you must renounce the hidden things of darkness. Every day you have to cleanse yourself of all the sins of the flesh. Daily take up your cross and follow Him. You say, "Oh, pastor, I get so tired." You must do it every day or you won't make it. Brother, you will be off and on, up and down, hot and cold, for the rest of your life. You will be running up and down aisles for the rest of your life, sitting in churches like a lot of people do at Calvary Baptist and other churches. You will be cold, dead, and intellectual, having all the answers from the Bible, but no answers in your life. You will have no joy, no peace, and no fruitfulness in your life—you have all the answers in your mouth, but nothing in your life. I die daily. Daily I read the Word of God. Daily I take up my cross and follow Him.

Pray—Daily

Every day you should set aside a time of prayer. Psalm 86:3 says, "Be merciful unto me, O Lord: for I cry unto thee daily." There are times when Christians go day after day after day, and all they ever do is thank the Lord for their food, and sometimes they don't even do that. There is no real thankfulness in the canned prayer they say at dinner time. "Thank You for the food, Lord." Psalm 88:9 says, "Mine eye mourneth by reason of affliction: Lord, I have called daily upon thee, I have stretched out my hands unto thee." First Thessalonians 5:17 says, "Pray without ceasing." What do I have to do to have that life? Jesus Christ says, "I am come that they might have life, and that they might have it more abundantly" (John 10:10).

Praise the Lord—Daily

Psalm 119:164 says, "Seven times a day do I praise thee." How many times a day do you praise the Lord? The Bible says, "Rejoice in the Lord alway, and again I say rejoice" (Phil. 4:4). Satan never has a hold on a praising Christian. Satan took away all that Job had, and Job got on his knees and worshiped and said, "The Lord gave, and the Lord hath taken away; blessed be the name of the Lord" (Job 1:21). Can you breathe without any effort? Praise the Lord. Can you see your children and your wife? Praise the Lord. Do you have a heart that beats and you don't have to take pills for it? Praise the Lord. Do you have legs that can walk? Praise the Lord. "Seven times a day do I praise thee" (Ps. 119:164). Get on your knees and praise the Lord for His goodness.

Depend upon God—Daily

In Luke 11:2–3 "[Christ] said unto them, When ye pray, say, Our Father which art in heaven, Hallowed be thy name. Thy kingdom come. Thy will be done, as in heaven, so in earth. Give us day by day our daily bread." It comes easy for me to sit down and put the Bible together and get a sermon ready. I can even talk to people instantly concerning the Word by using all the talents that the Lord has given me. Self-sufficiency was born in me the day that I was born. Self-dependence and self-glorification were also there the day I was born. In preachers as well as anybody else, there is a need to go to God to say, "Oh, Lord, it will just be a message, if You're not in it." Unless the Lord build the house, they labor in vain that build it. Unless the Lord guards the city, they watch it but in vain. We need to know that everything that we are and have came from God. All God has to do is whisper, and we don't have any of it. When Nebuchadnezzar walked upon the great wall of Babylon, he said, "Is not this great Babylon that I have built?" (Dan. 4:30). That very night he went insane; God took his mind from him. Jesus tells the story of the rich man who planted his ground and the ground brought forth abundantly. He said, "I know what I'll do. I'll tear down my barns, and I'll build bigger barns, and I'll say to my soul, 'Soul, eat and drink and be merry.' God said, 'Thou fool, this night thy soul shall be required of thee'" (Luke 12:20). Daily depend upon Him. I come to God and thank Him for all that He gives me *daily.*

Confess Sin—Daily

First John 1:9 says, "If we confess our sins, he is faithful and just to forgive us our sins, and to cleanse us from all unrighteousness." He cleanses us as often as we ask. We need a daily confession of our sins to God that we might be daily cleansed of our sins. Psalm 32:5 says, "I acknowledged my sin unto thee, and mine iniquity have I not hid. I said, I will confess my transgressions unto the Lord; and thou forgavest the iniquity of my sin." Proverbs 28:13

says, "He that covereth his sins shall not prosper: but whoso confesseth and forsaketh them shall have mercy."

Every day I confess my sins. You know something? As soon as you give your life to Christ and say, "Lord, I'm going to start doing what it takes to have a daily abundant, Christian, Spirit-filled life," some sin will come into your mind and into you life. What do you do? Get it out—as soon as it comes, get rid of it. Treat it like a cancer, treat it like a hot poker, and get rid of it. Daily, hourly, confess your sins to the Lord. You say, "Pastor, I gave my life to Christ, two, three, four times, and it just does not work."

You know why it didn't work? It is because you don't do it every day. You need to die every morning. You do it two or three mornings, get tired of it, and stop dying. You don't read your Bible. You try that three or four mornings, and start dying (you really start dying then). You pray once in a while, and you expect God to give you a victorious life. The Bible says, "Thanks be unto God, which *always* causeth us to triumph" (II Cor. 2:14). Who always gives us the victory? When is this always true? It is true when we are daily doing the things that God tells us to do. God allows us to triumph, shows us to have joy unspeakable and full of glory, allows us to have an abundant life, and allows us to have victory.

Perform Your Vows—Daily

Psalm 61:8 says, "So will I sing praises unto thy name for ever, that I may daily perform my vows." All those promises that you make to God about your children, about your life, you need to *daily* perform your vows. Ecclesiastes 5:1–6 is the most definitive passage in the Word of God on vows and promises that we make to God.

> Keep thy foot when thou goest to the house of God, and be more ready to hear, than to give the sacrifice of fools: for they consider not that they do evil. Be not rash with thy mouth, and let not thine heart be hasty to utter any thing before God: for God is in heaven, and thou upon earth: therefore let thy words be few. For a dream cometh through the multitude of business: and a fool's voice is known by multitude of words. When thou vowest a vow unto God, defer not to pay it: for he hath no pleasure in fools: pay that which thou hast vowed. Better is it that thou

shouldest not vow, than that thou shouldest vow and not pay. Suffer not thy mouth to cause thy flesh to sin: neither say thou before the angel, that it was an error: wherefore should God be angry at thy voice, and destroy the work of thine hands?

Everyone is looking for some wonderful, staggering secret of God to give him a good Christian life. God is a very practical God. He says that there are eight things to do, and if you do them every single day, and never stop doing them, you will have a victorious Christian life. Ruskin said, "A habit is a cable. You weave a thread of it every day, until at last you cannot break it, either a bad one, or a good one." You should give your life totally and completely to Christ. A lot of folks come down the aisles saying, "I want to give my life to Christ," but they have never forsaken their sin, their sinful ways, their sinful friends. They have been sorry, but not sorry enough to repent. They wonder why their Christian life never takes hold. You must first of all have a complete cleansing and a breaking before Almighty God. Once you have had that every single day, you die, and let Him live. If every single day you read the Word of God systematically, if every single day you take up your cross and follow Him, He will never lead you into compromise or sin of any kind. Every single day you need to plead with the God of heaven, every single day praise His holy name and depend upon Him. You must confess your sins and every day pay your vows, and the Bible says you will never fall.

In the New Testament we have these examples. First of all, we read in Acts 2 about the first people that ever got saved. Listen to what they did in Acts 2:41–47.

> Then they that gladly received his word were baptized; and the same day there were added unto them about three thousand souls. And they continued steadfastly in the apostles' doctrine and fellowship, and in breaking of bread, and in prayers. And fear came upon every soul: and many wonders and signs were done by the apostles. And all that believed were together. . . . And they, continuing daily with one accord in the temple, and breaking bread from house to house, did eat their meat with gladness and singleness of heart. Praising God, and having favour with all

the people. And the Lord added to the church daily such as should be saved.

God is a *daily* God. He isn't the God of yesterday or the God of tomorrow. Jesus Christ and God are the God and Savior of today. Today is the only day you have of the rest of your life. You can never be sure about tomorrow. God does not expect us to do something great, say something great, learn something great, or accomplish something great. *God never said we had to be successful*; God only said we had to be faithful. If you will be faithful unto death, God will give you the crown of life. If every single day you will just do these things, the Bible says you will never fall. You will always be victorious, always triumph, have joy unspeakable and full of glory, have an abundant life, and be saved from this present evil world. Are these hypothetical or idealistic standards that God has set forth? They are for you and me today. We can have them in our Christian life.

Thousands upon thousands have said to me, "Pastor, how can I do it?" When I tell them, they go away very sorrowful because they want an easy solution to a complex problem. They want me to say, "Just memorize this verse and get down and say a prayer, and every-thing will be all right." *It won't be.* Salvation is a once-for-all deci-sion, but the Christian life involves choices every day.

As soon as I got saved, my four friends, Dick and Martha Mitchell and Frank and Joy Forrest, took me under their wings and with much patience prayed for me daily. They spent many hours teaching me the Word of God. Most of their training was just an-swering my endless questions. They never said to me, "Bob, you must stop smoking, stop drinking, stop cussing, and stop fighting." No, they just prayed and answered my questions.

I never took another drink from then until now. I will never forget the day I asked Frank why I was the only one in the church that smoked? I was a cigar smoker when I went to bed, and I got up smoking. He said to me, "Bob, that isn't true, because the smokers in our church just hide it." My question obviously was "Why hide it?" I told Frank to show me in the Bible that it is sinful and wrong for the believer. His answer was perfect for me. He said, "Are you sure that you are saved?" and I answered yes. His second question was "Is Jesus Christ the Lord of your life?" I assured him He was. The third question was "Is Christ your example?" and I again assured him He was. Frank's fourth question really got to me. "Bob, can you imagine your Lord and your example walking down the streets in Jerusalem with a cigar in His mouth?"

Wow, what a question! By that very question I knew it was wrong to smoke cigars. I had two boxes left of my usual three that I purchased each payday, and I got rid of them. All my division laughed at me when I said that I had smoked my last cigar. They all waited to see when I would take up the habit again. Because of God's grace, I never smoked another cigar.

My battle against the flesh was just getting started when I put smoking and drinking out of my life. It didn't hurt very much to get the victory over them. But *cussing* was another story. My, oh my, what a battle and what a struggle. Most believers can have victory over most of their sins, but they have some that they carry with them through their Christian life. It seems that total victory never comes. You must remember that in the military you don't go home after your eight hours to a mother or a wife. No, you live twenty-four hours a day with the men you work with, and in the service cussing is a way of life. So I prayed and fasted and could go a day or two without cussing. Sometimes I cussed silently under my breath so no one heard me, but *God did.* That was *fifty-five* years ago. I will never forget the last time I lost my cool and cussed.

We were having Admiral's Inspection, and believe me that is all-important in the navy. No one walks on a wet deck. I happened to be swabbing a deck and several sailors came by and, because they knew I was saved, walked on my newly swabbed deck. Before I knew it, I cussed them out, and of course they laughed at me. They also said, "You call yourself a Christian!" *I was crushed* because I thought I had victory over cussing. I finished my job and found a small room where I knew I could be alone. I poured out my heart to the Lord. I said, "Lord, I am not a good Christian; I've tried every way I know how, and I can't get victory over cussing." I pleaded with the Lord for help and forgiveness. How could I tell those lost sailors they needed to repent and accept Christ as their Savior when I cussed?

I was a hypocrite in their eyes. It looked to them as though I couldn't have control of my sin; how could I show them how to get saved? I remember sitting in that small, dark room saying to the Lord, "Lord, this is it; I either get victory over this sin or I quit today." And that day I learned another principle from the Lord. Sometimes we pray, but not sincerely, or we pray halfheartedly. When a child of God prays in desperation, it works. It is like Jacob wrestling with the Lord. Genesis 32:24–30 says,

> And Jacob was left alone; and there wrestled a man with him until the breaking of the day. And when he saw that he prevailed not against him, he touched the hollow of his thigh; and the hollow of Jacob's thigh was out of joint, as he wrestled with him. And he said, let me go, for the day breaketh. And he said, I will not let thee go, except thou bless me. And he said unto him, What is thy name? And he said, Jacob. And he said, Thy name shall be called no more Jacob, but Israel: for as a prince hast thou power with God and with men, and hast prevailed. And Jacob asked him, and said, Tell me, I pray thee, thy name. And he said, Wherefore is it that thou dost ask after my name? And he blessed him there. And Jacob called the name of the place Peniel: for I have seen God face to face, and my life is preserved.

Jacob had spent a lifetime getting his own way by hook or by crook. By outright lying, he hurt everyone he met. If there is anyone in the Bible that is a picture of the carnal believer, or the believer who lives under the power of the flesh, or the believer who stands in the middle of the road, or the believer who believes God did not intend for him to be *obedient, dedicated, separated, surrendered, filled by the Holy Spirit*, it is Jacob. That's exactly how Jacob believed and lived, *until he came face to face with God.* Jacob had prayed before, but now he prayed desperately. Jacob said he would not let go until God blessed him. He became a changed man. He now had power with God and man. Desperate praying is not the best; we ought not to wait until the situation becomes desperate before we do something about it. Romans 7 is the chief New Testament passage on the flesh because it shows the believer the real enemy.

From that day on I had victory over cussing. In your own case it may not be cussing. It may be a lust for things, immorality, exalting yourself for a position, being power hungry, lying, or anything else that comes before the Lord. When your strength comes to an end and you become desperate, He will hear you, and you will be delivered.

For a new believer with no one to lead him, it takes time reading and praying to understand the battles with the flesh. However, with God's good blessing, all things are possible. Here are some of the things that I have learned:

1. The flesh is the human body, what we are at birth, a living man totally controlled by physical appetites. Man is born into a human family with no ability to be spiritual. The reason man is so helplessly lost is that God is a Spirit; and to know Him, man needs to be re-created, or born again, into a spirit being. Man has tried a thousand ways to know God, to worship God, and to get God's approval. All to no avail. What Christ did not do to the lost when He saved them was to renew the old nature. The Lord did not restore the old nature. Christ did not make a second chance to please Him. The Lord did not die to repair the old nature.

2. The Bible says in Galatians 5:17, "For the flesh lusteth against the Spirit, and the Spirit against the flesh; and these are contrary the one to the other: so that ye cannot do the things that ye would." The flesh keeps us from obeying the Word of God. In Romans 8:13 we read, "For if ye live after the flesh, ye shall die: but if ye through the Spirit do mortify the deeds of the body, ye shall live."

3. The control of the flesh is found in I Corinthians 9:27. "But I keep under my body, and bring it into subjection: lest that by any means, when I have preached to others, I myself should be a castaway." Romans 6:12 says, "Let not sin therefore reign in your mortal body, that ye should obey it in the lusts thereof."

John 6:63 says, "It is the Spirit that quickeneth; the flesh profiteth nothing: the words that I speak unto you, they are spirit, and they are life."

4. Some examples of people who gave in to the flesh are Adam and Eve, David, Samson, and Peter at the fire and at Antioch. Galatians 2:11 says, "But when Peter was come to Antioch, I withstood him to the face, because he was to be blamed." *And, of course, you could add yourself and me to the list.* Every believer has the testimony of the power of the flesh. All of us bear its scars.

Too often we believe Satan's lies, one of these being that believers can't commit really bad sins but only small, innocent ones. H. S. Miller in *The Christian Workers' Manual* (N.p.: Christian Publications, page 3436) says some startling things about the believer and sin.

He says there are in the New Testament no less than 21 lists of sins, with a total of 103 different sins. If I were to ask you how many you have committed this year, could you name at least 25 or 50 sins by name?

One of the great problems in Christianity is our appalling ignorance of what sin is and our refusal to call it by its biblical name. The world calls it a fib, but the Bible calls it a lie. The world calls it a little sin, but the Bible calls all sin, sin. The world calls it abortion; the Bible calls it murder. The world calls it safe sex, but the Bible calls it adultery. The world calls it overeating, but the Bible calls it gluttony. If we do not know the names of sin, then we could be committing many of them ignorantly. I checked on Dr. Miller's "Twenty-one lists of sins in the New Testament" and found him to be perfectly right, so let's look at his lists.

1. Seven that come from the natural heart and defile. "But those things which proceed out of the mouth come forth from the heart; and they defile the man. For out of the heart proceed evil thoughts, murders, adulteries, fornications, thefts, false witness, blasphemies: these are the things which defile a man:

but to eat with unwashen hands defileth not a man" (Matt. 15:18–20).

2. Thirteen that come from the natural heart and defile. "For from within, out of the heart of men, proceed evil thoughts, adulteries, fornications, murders, thefts, covetousness, wickedness, deceit, lasciviousness, an evil eye, blasphemy, pride, foolishness: all these evil things come from within, and defile the man" (Mark 7:21–23).

3. Twenty-three that bring the judgment of God. "Being filled with all unrighteousness, fornication, wickedness, covetousness, maliciousness; full of envy, murder, debate, deceit, malignity; whisperers, backbiters, haters of God, despiteful, proud, boasters, inventors of evil things, disobedient to parents, without understanding, covenantbreakers, without natural affection, implacable, unmerciful: who knowing the judgment of God, that they which commit such things are worthy of death, not only do the same, but have pleasure in them that do them" (Rom. 1:29–32).

4. Seven that Christians must not do. "Let us walk honestly, as in the day; not in rioting and drunkenness, not in chambering and wantonness, not in strife and envying. But put ye on the Lord Jesus Christ, and make not provision for the flesh, to fulfil the lusts thereof" (Rom. 13:13–14).

5. Six with which Christians must not associate. "I wrote unto you in an epistle not to company with fornicators: yet not altogether with the fornicators of this world, or with the covetous, or extortioners, or with idolaters; for then must ye needs go out of the world. But now I have written unto you not to keep company, if any man that is called a brother be a fornicator, or covetous, or an idolater, or a railer, or a drunkard, or an extortioner; with such an one no not to eat" (I Cor. 5:9–11).

6. Ten that bar from the kingdom of God. "Know ye not that the unrighteous shall not inherit the kingdom of God? Be not deceived: neither fornicators, nor idolaters, nor adulterers, nor effeminate, nor abusers of themselves with mankind, nor

thieves, nor covetous, nor drunkards, nor revilers, nor extortioners, shall inherit the kingdom of God" (I Cor. 6:9–10).

7. Eleven from which Christians must turn away. "For I fear, lest, when I come, I shall not find you such as I would, and that I shall be found unto you such as ye would not: lest there be debates, envyings, wraths, strifes, backbitings, whisperings, swellings, tumults: and lest, when I come again, my God will humble me among you, and that I shall bewail many which have sinned already, and have not repented of the uncleanness and fornication and lasciviousness which they have committed" (II Cor. 12:20–21).

8. Seventeen that bar from the kingdom of God. "Now the works of the flesh are manifest, which are these: adultery, fornication, uncleanness, lasciviousness, idolatry, witchcraft, hatred, variance, emulations, wrath, strife, seditions, heresies, envyings, murders, drunkenness, revellings, and such like: of the which I tell you before, as I have also told you in time past, that they which do such things shall not inherit the kingdom of God" (Gal. 5:19–21).

9. Nine in which the unsaved live and in which Christians must not live. "This I say therefore, and testify in the Lord, that ye henceforth walk not as other Gentiles walk, in the vanity of their mind, having the understanding darkened, being alienated from the life of God through the ignorance that is in them, because of the blindness of their heart: who being past feeling have given themselves over unto lasciviousness, to work all uncleanness with greediness" (Eph. 4:17–19).

10. Nine that Christians must put away. "Wherefore putting away lying, speak every man truth with his neighbour: for we are members one of another. . . . Let him that stole steal no more: but rather let him labour, working with his hands the thing which is good, that he may have to give to him that needeth. Let no corrupt communication proceed out of your mouth, but that which is good to the use of edifying, that it may minister grace unto the hearers. . . . Let all bitterness, and wrath, and

anger, and clamour, and evil speaking, be put away from you, with all malice" (Eph. 4:25, 28–29, 31).

11. Six that must not be named as existing among Christians. "But fornication, and all uncleanness, or covetousness, let it not be once named among you, as becometh saints; neither filthiness, nor foolish talking, nor jesting, which are not convenient: but rather giving of thanks" (Eph. 5:3–4).

12. Four that bar from the kingdom of God and of Christ and that bring the wrath of God. "For this ye know, that no whoremonger, nor unclean person, nor covetous man, who is an idolater, hath any inheritance in the kingdom of Christ and of God. Let no man deceive you with vain words: for because of these things cometh the wrath of God upon the children of disobedience" (Eph. 5:5–6).

13. Six that Christians must mortify and that bring the wrath of God. "Mortify therefore your members which are upon the earth; fornication, uncleanness, inordinate affection, evil concupiscence, and covetousness, which is idolatry: for which things' sake the wrath of God cometh on the children of disobedience" (Col. 3:5–6).

14. Six that Christians must put off. "But now ye also put off all these; anger, wrath, malice, blasphemy, filthy communication out of your mouth. Lie not one to another, seeing that ye have put off the old man with his deeds" (Col. 3:8–9).

15. Fourteen for which the law was given. "Knowing this, that the law is not made for a righteous man, but for the lawless and disobedient, for the ungodly and for sinners, for unholy and profane, for murderers of fathers and murderers of mothers, for manslayers. For whoremongers, for them that defile themselves with mankind, for menstealers, for liars, for perjured persons, and if there be any other thing that is contrary to sound doctrine" (I Tim. 1:9–10).

16. Nineteen from which Christians must turn away. "This know also, that in the last days perilous times shall come. For men shall be lovers of their own selves, covetous, boasters, proud,

blasphemers, disobedient to parents, unthankful, unholy. Without natural affection, trucebreakers, false accusers, incontinent, fierce, despisers of those that are good, traitors, heady, highminded, lovers of pleasures more than lovers of God; having a form of godliness, but denying the power thereof: from such turn away" (II Tim. 3:1–5).

17. Nine from which Christians are saved. "For we ourselves also were sometimes foolish, disobedient, deceived, serving divers lusts and pleasures, living in malice and envy, hateful, and hating one another. But after that the kindness and love of God our Saviour toward man appeared, not by works of righteousness which we have done, but according to his mercy he saved us, by the washing of regeneration, and renewing of the Holy Ghost" (Titus 3:3–5).

18. Five that Christians must lay aside. "Wherefore laying aside all malice, and all guile, and hypocrisies, and envies, and all evil speakings" (I Pet. 2:1).

19. Seven sins of the flesh in which Christians used to live. "That he no longer should live the rest of his time in the flesh to the lusts of men, but to the will of God. For the time past of our life may suffice us to have wrought the will of the Gentiles, when we walked in lasciviousness, lusts, excess of wine, revellings, banquetings, and abominable idolatries. Wherein they think it strange that ye run not with them to the same excess of riot, speaking evil of you" (I Pet. 4:2–4).

20. Eight that condemn to the lake of fire. "But the fearful, and unbelieving, and the abominable, and murderers, and whoremongers, and sorcerers, and idolaters, and all liars, shall have their part in the lake which burneth with fire and brimstone: which is the second death" (Rev. 21:8).

21. Six that bar from the tree of life and the Holy City. "For without are dogs, and sorcerers, and whoremongers, and murderers, and idolaters, and whosoever loveth and maketh a lie" (Rev. 22:15).

The total is 202. Some are found in more than one list, but there are 103 different sins in the 21 lists. There are several major lessons we need to see and learn.

Don't call by any other name that which God calls sin.

What man says	What God says
overeating	gluttony
fibbing	lying
borrowing	stealing
lusting	adultery
hate	murder

Notice God says we must confess our sins (plural). First John 1:9 says, "If we confess our sins, he is faithful and just to forgive us our sins." Don't take the offense out of sin. Romans 7:13 says, "That sin by the commandment might become exceeding sinful."

Look at the lists again and notice what God calls sin: murder, adultery, fornication, theft, betrayal, lying. Add to this list rape, abortion, incest, and idolatry, which we as believers agree with the Holy Spirit are evil. But the Holy Spirit adds many more sins that many believers ignore or treat with disdain: *envy, debate, backbiting, deceit, covenant breaking, pride, whispering, boasting, being unmerciful, bitterness, self love, unthankfulness, headiness, loving pleasures, and foolishness.*

As you fight the battle with the three enemies of your soul, Satan has a goal for every man, woman, boy, and girl. If you are lost, Satan will do everything in his power to keep you lost. If you are a believer, he will use that same power to make you a hypocrite, a carnal believer, a backslider, a stumbling block. I believe it is safe to say that most believers are losing the battle of the flesh. *The world, the Devil, and the flesh will cause you to treat sin lightly instead of asking God to make sin exceedingly sinful.*

It would be great if sanctification were like salvation. In salvation we hear the gospel, believe the gospel, and finally receive the gospel. To hear and obey is to believe that Christ died for us and rose again the third day. We finally accept Him as our personal

Savior. First Corinthians 15:3–4 says, "For I delivered unto you first of all that which I also received, how that Christ died for our sins according to the scriptures; and that he was buried, and that he rose again the third day according to the scriptures." We never have to get saved again. Romans 8:38–39 says, "For I am persuaded, that neither death, nor life, nor angels, nor principalities, nor powers, nor things present, nor things to come, nor height, nor depth, nor any other creature, shall be able to separate us from the love of God, which is in Christ Jesus our Lord." *The Lord does it all.*

However, in sanctification, *it is God and you.* You hear such words as James 4:7, "Submit yourselves therefore to God. Resist the devil, and he will flee from you." Hebrews 12:1 says, "Run with patience." First John 1:7 says, "Walk in the light." Philippians 3:13–14 says, "I count. . . . I press."

First Corinthians 16:13 says, "Watch ye, stand fast in the faith, quit you." First Peter 1:15 says, "Be ye holy . . ." First Timothy 5:22 tells us to keep ourselves pure. James 1:27 teaches us to "keep [ourselves] unspotted from the world." First Corinthians 15:58 says, "Be ye stedfast, unmoveable."

Salvation is for one time, one place, and it is finished forever. You can't add to it, and you can't subtract from it. Once you have received Christ as your Savior, *it is finished.*

Sanctification starts at salvation and only stops at death or the Rapture. Sanctification is *the battle of the flesh.* As salvation is fought only once, the battle of the flesh is fought daily. The battle is new every time you wake up. If the battle of the flesh were easy, every believer would be victorious. But the battle is to be fought and won when God gives to the believer a command. He will always provide for the journey. Look at Israel in the Old Testament getting Pharaoh to let them go. Then the Red Sea had to be crossed, then the bitter waters of Marah, and from there to the battle with the Amalekites. For forty years they murmured and complained. They wanted to kill Moses, but finally after forty years they came to the Promised Land.

CHIEF

The battle against the flesh is fought daily. There are no short-cuts. The Lord gives the commands. The Lord shows the way. The Epistles show how it is done. Like manna that had to be collected daily, so our battle is fought daily. Please notice the ingredients:

- Galatians 5:16—Walk in the control of the Spirit.
- Ephesians 2:2—Walk not according to the course of this world.
- Ephesians 2:1—Walk as His workmanship.
- Ephesians 4:1—Walk worthy.
- Ephesians 4:17—Walk not as the lost.
- Ephesians 5:2—Walk in love.
- Ephesians 5:8—Walk as children of the light.
- Colossians 4:5—Walk in wisdom toward them that are without.
- Ephesians 5:15—Walk circumspectly, with caution.

THE BATTLE
AGAINST THE MASONIC LODGE

A Mason is a member of a major secret society called Free and Accepted Masons. Among lodges, Freemasonry is the oldest and largest lodge. The Masonic Lodge for women is called the Eastern Star and for youth DeMolay.

There are many lodges and none of them is a friend to Christianity. The difference between other lodges and Masonry is that Masonry is a religious lodge. The Masonic Lodge is involved in many good things such as the Shriners Hospitals for Children. But we must remember that good works do not make any man or organization righteous.

HOW I WAS INTRODUCED TO THE MASONIC LODGE

I was saved January 19, 1948, and married Marjorie Brooks a year later on January 22, 1949. After I spent a six-month cruise in the Mediterranean Sea, I petitioned for shore duty in Philadelphia. My request for this was approved, and I could be with my wife. But there was another important thing I could do and did do—enroll in an evening Bible institute. I ran a tugboat all day and went to school two nights a week at the Philadelphia Bible Institute. I wanted to get on with my education and get my GED since I had only finished sixth grade before enlisting in the navy.

CHIEF

While attending the institute, I took a course entitled Heresy Exposed. I was shocked because I had always been taught that the Masons were just a harmless club for men. But as I studied, I knew I had to have a serious talk with my pastor. He had graduated from the same institute, and both of us had had this course. We had two boards at our church, deacons and trustees. Of the sixteen officers, fifteen were members of the Masonic Lodge in good standing.

I spent almost a whole day debating with my pastor, and the thing that shocked me was that he kept agreeing with me. I said to him over and over, "Pastor, how can you keep on agreeing with me that the Masonic Lodge is pure heresy and no true born again believer should be caught dead in it if the board members of our church are members?"

His answer was "I don't want to rock the boat. I don't want to be kicked out of this church. There are more important things to be fighting over." To which I replied, "Nothing is more important than *obedience*." Deuteronomy 11:27 says, "A blessing, if ye obey the commandments of the Lord your God, which I command you this day."

Another thing he said was that these men, though they were members of the Masonic Lodge, were good and godly men. I guess the problem then was with what the pastor felt was good and godly. His explanation was really just an excuse to have the men he wanted on the boards. Once you have read the doctrines and moral standards of the bloody oaths the Masons take with hands on the Bible, I believe that you too will come to the conclusion that *no blood-bought child of God should be in the Masonic Lodge.*

I told my pastor that I wanted to speak to the board members and challenge them to withdraw from the lodge. He objected but reluctantly let me do it. You could have cut the atmosphere of the meeting with a knife. I tried to explain to the members that I had not called this meeting to condemn them or to embarrass them. But before I could speak, the chairman went into a long and fiery tirade telling me that I was a know-it-all, a busybody, a young punk who was wet behind the ears, a showoff, and many other names, too. I got absolutely nowhere with the board members. I marveled that these born-again men were all in favor of putting the lodge above the constitution of the church.

After a long debate, I finally said to the chairman, "Mr. Chairman, just answer me one question, and I will leave." He replied, "What is your question?" "While you were taking the oaths for the different degrees of the Lodge, and there are thirty-two degrees, after you learned the secrets of each degree, did you lay your hand on the Bible, God's Holy Word, and swear in the name of God? Could you take a bloody oath such as the penalty assumed by every man who takes the entered apprentice obligation?"

Well, *that did it,* and I was ordered out of the room. My pastor did not say one word on my behalf, and I knew that my days at that church were numbered.

As soon as my wife and I reached Lansdale, one of my first acts as pastor was to rewrite our constitution. In the constitution I placed these words: *No candidate can become a member who is a member of any secret society such as, Communism, Masonry, etc.* John 18:19–20 says, "The high priest then asked Jesus of his disciples, and of his doctrine. Jesus answered him, I spake openly to the world; I ever taught in the synagogue, and in the temple, whither the Jews always resort; and in *secret* have I said nothing."

Immediately war was declared in Lansdale. Again I was told almost the same as the Lansdale Ministerium had told me. "Who are you and how did you get here? Where did you come from? You will never succeed in Lansdale." Needless to say, as soon as some Masonic members started getting saved, the big shots in the lodge were upset. It reminded me of Nehemiah 2:10, "When Sanballat the Horonite, and Tobiah the servant, the Ammonite, heard of it, it grieved them exceedingly that there was come a man to seek the welfare of the children of Israel."

A young man got saved and asked if he could join our church. My answer was that he could as long as he was not a member of a secret organization like the Masonic Lodge. He was honestly shocked. He said to me, "Pastor, the Masonic Lodge is the greatest organization in this whole country. Please explain it to me." My answer to him was "No, I'll not try to explain it to you, but let's try an experiment." I handed him six gospel tracts and told him what I wanted him to do when he went to the next meeting. "After the first part of the meeting is over and you go to another part of the lodge for fellowship, playing cards, checkers, or Ping Pong, sit down and play some kind of game with a small group of them. I want you to pass out these tracts. Don't be loud or insulting. Be kind, concerned, and friendly. If you can pass out all five without being rebuked or told to stop, I'll join the lodge." I knew very well he would be stopped. The reason I was so sure is that Masons will not tolerate any sectarian views in the lodge. That was Sunday, and by Wednesday he was back to see me with a very long face. He cried and said that he could not believe it. He told me he had built his whole life around the lodge. Many of his family were in it. He told me that he had done exactly as I had told him to do. He offered the first tract to a young man his own age and was told immediately that that was forbidden. A Mason is to leave his sectarianism outside the door. He said, "Pastor, I'm out, and I'll write a letter first thing tomorrow."

If a believer is ignorant of the wickedness of the Masonic Lodge, as I was, he at least has an excuse. All around us we hear only how great and good and generous they are. And as a matter of fact, they do much good, but good works will not take a person to heaven. The Masons really do believe that *character determines destiny*. The sad fact is that many Christians are members of the Masonic Lodge.

If a person is a blood-bought child of God, he has no excuse for being a member. Christian pastors who are Masonic members are also without excuse. When joining the lodge, they lay their hand on the Bible and swear a bloody oath in the name of God . If they are saved, the moment they hear the oath they should separate from that lodge.

THE OFFENSIVE TEACHING OF THE LODGE

Just what does the Masonic Lodge believe and teach that is so offensive? First, the names and titles given to their leaders are offensive.

- Worshipful Master
- Grand Pontiff
- Prince of Mercy
- Sublime Master Elect
- Prince of the Tabernacle
- Sovereign Grand Inspector General

Only the leaders of the lodge would have enough gall to call themselves by the names of deity, using the titles of our Lord Jesus Christ. This is blasphemy, and may God have mercy on their lost souls.

The lodge voices great faith in the Bible, but please do not believe their claim is true. James L. Holly, M.D., president of Mission and Ministry to Men, has written a three-volume set of books about the lodge and the Southern Baptist Convention. These volumes are of tremendous value to Fundamentalist churches. In volume I, pages 88–90, we read,

> The most common quotation in Masonic literature about the Bible is that of Joseph Fort Newton from his book, *The Men's House*. This book was published by the Masonic Service Association of the United States and was originally copyrighted in 1923. Newton stated:

> "And yet, like everything else in Masonry, the Bible, so rich in symbolism, is itself a symbol—that is, a part taken for the whole. It is a sovereign symbol of the Book of Faith; the Will of God as man has learned it in the midst of the years—that perpetual revelation of himself, which God is making to mankind in every land and every age. Thus, by the very honor which Masonry pays to the Bible, it teaches us to revere every book of faith in which men find help for today and hope for the morrow, joining hands with the man of Islam as he takes oath on the Koran, and with the Hindu as he makes covenant with God upon the book that he loves best.

"For Masonry knows, what so many forget, that religions are many, but Religion is one—perhaps we may say one thing, but that one thing includes everything—the life of God in the soul of man, and the duty and hope of man which proceed from His essential character. Therefore it invites to its altar men of all faiths, knowing that, if they use different names for 'the Nameless One of a hundred names,' they are yet praying to the one God and Father of all; knowing, also, that while they read different volumes, they are in fact reading the same vast Book of the Faith of Man as revealed in the struggle and sorrow of the race in its quest of God. So that, great and noble as the Bible is, Masonry sees it as a symbol of the eternal Book of the Will of God.

"None the less, much as we honor every book of faith in which any man has found courage to lift his hand above the night that covers him and lay hold of the mighty Hand of God, with us the Bible is supreme. What Homer was to the Greeks, what the Koran is to the Arabs, that, and much more, the grand Old Bible is to us."

The denial, not only of the inerrancy of Scripture, but of the uniqueness of it, cuts at the very heart of the message of Jesus Christ. This is the message of the Masonic Lodge: Jesus Christ was one Savior, but not the only One; the Bible is one book of the Law, but not the only one. In a democratic republic, any individual has the right to believe that; in a Southern Baptist church anyone who does must declare that they are not a Southern Baptist.

We teach a belief in no particular creed, as we teach unbelief in none. In all religions there is a basis of Truth; in all there are fragments at least of pure Morality. All that teach the cardinal tenets of Masonry, we respect; all teachers and reformers of mankind, we admire and revere.

We do not tell the Hebrew that the Messiah whom he expects was born in Bethlehem nearly two thousand years ago, and substituted a better faith in the place of the Law of Moses. And as little do we tell the sincere Christian that Jesus of Nazareth was but a man like us. . . . Masonry, of no one age, belongs to all time; or no one religion, it finds its great truths in all (*The Little Masonic Library*, Vol. V, p. 46).

Dr. John R. Rice, founder and editor of *The Sword of the Lord*, from Murfreesboro, Tennessee, wrote a book entitled *Lodges Examined by the Bible*. On page 35 he states, "The Bible of the lodges may be the Koran or any so-called 'Sacred Book' of heathen religions." I copied the following statement from the *Encyclopedia of Masonry,* page 104, in the Scottish Rite Cathedral in Dallas a few years ago:

> The Bible is properly called a greater light of Masonry, for from the center of the lodge it pours forth upon the East, the West, and the South its refulgent rays of Divine truth. The Bible is used among Masons as a symbol of the will of God, however it may be expressed, and therefore, whatever to any people expresses that will, may be used as a substitute for the Bible in the Masonic Lodge. Thus, in a lodge consisting entirely of Jews the Old Testament alone may be placed upon the altar, and Turkish Masons make use of the Koran. Whether it be the Gospels to the Christians, the Pentateuch to the Israelite, the Koran to the Muslim, the Vedas to the Brahman, it everywhere Masonically conveys the same idea—that of the symbolism of the Divine will revealed to man.

Masons, then, regard the Bible as only one of *many sacred books,* the one as good as the other, for Masonic purposes. A Mohammedan can be as good a Mason as a Christian preacher. The Hindu religion fits in as well with Masonry.

SOME MASONIC CLAIMS

- The lodges claim about four million members.
- They claim that they were started with the building of Solomon's temple.
- They claim that they are not a religion.

But after a close look at their beliefs and practices, a person must conclude that that is exactly what they are.

To the vast majority of the Masons that I have met the lodge is first. There is no way that the lodge can prove their devotion to the Word of God. They put together Islam, Buddhism, liberalism, and Judaism. The only group missing is hated Fundamentalism. Rest assured that the Bible is a strange book to most Masons.

THE MASONS AND SECRECY

As a candidate climbs the ladder in the Masonic Lodge, he learns very quickly that at each level he advances to, he is given secrets that he must *swear with a bloody oath never to divulge.* This would have serious consequences.

But our Lord said in John 18:20, "Jesus answered him, I spake openly to the world; I ever taught in the synagogue, and in the temple, whither the Jews always resort; and in *secret have I said nothing.*" In Ecclesiastes 12:14 we read, "For God shall bring every work into judgment, with every secret thing, whether it be good, or whether it be evil." Then in Romans 2:16 we read, "In the day when God shall judge the secrets of men by Jesus Christ according to my gospel."

THE MASONS AND BLOODY OATHS

On pages 22 and 23 of Dr. Rice's book *Lodges Examined by the Bible* we read,

> The Penalties of Masonic Oaths are unchristian, blood-thirsty, and murderous. Read again the penalty assumed by every man who takes the Entered Apprentice Obligation: [Binding myself under no less a penalty than that of having my throat cut across, my tongue torn out by its roots, and buried in the rough sands of the sea at low-water mark, where the tide ebbs and flows twice in twenty-four hours, should I ever knowingly or willingly violate this my solemn oath and obligation as an Entered Apprentice Mason. So help me God, and keep me steadfast in the due performance of the same.] The second degree or Fellow-Craft Obligation has the following penalty: [Binding myself under no less a penalty than that of having my left breast torn open, my heart plucked out, and given as a prey to the wild beasts of the field and the fowls of the air.] The third or Master Mason's Obligation has this penalty: [Binding myself under no less a penalty than that of having my body severed in twain, and bowels taken from thence and burned to ashes, the ashes scattered to the four winds of heaven, so that no more trace or remembrance may be had of so vile and perjured a wretch as I, should I ever knowingly or willingly violate this my solemn obligation as a Master Mason. So help me God, and keep me steadfast in the due performance of the same.]
>
> The explanation says, [We are bound to cause their death, and take vengeance on the treason by the destruction of the traitors.]

Many times a Mason will deny what the lodge says. The thing you should do is to ask him for a Masonic Bible and have him turn to the very front. There you will find a clear and concise statement of faith.

A Masonic Creed

Found in the front pages of Masonic Bible:

"There is one God, the Father of all men.

The Holy Bible is the Great Light in Masonry, and the rule and guide for faith and practice.

Man is immortal.

Character determines destiny.

Love of man is, next to love of God, man's first duty.

Prayer, communion of man with God, is helpful.

Recognizing the impossibility of confining the teaching of Masonry to any fixed forms of expression, yet acknowledging the value of authoritative statements of fundamental principles."

THE FATHERHOOD OF GOD AND THE BROTHERHOOD OF MAN

Notice the heresy in the above creed. There is one God, the father of all men. John 8:44 says, "Ye are of your father the devil, and the lusts of your father ye will do. He was a murderer from the beginning, and abode not in the truth, because there is no truth in him. When he speaketh a lie, he speaketh of his own: for he is a liar, and the father of it."

According to the Bible all men are not "brothered," but are brothers only in Christ. God is the Creator of all men, *not the father of all men. You must do something to become the child of God.* Galatians 3:26 says, "For ye are all the children of God *by faith in Christ Jesus.*"

The lodge plan of salvation is in the front of every Masonic Bible. The beliefs of the lodge are spelled out clearly. Masons believe that *character determines destiny. Wow,* you can't speak more clearly than that. The religion of the lodge is the religion of good works and the religion of self-improvement.

CHIEF

In Psalm 37:23 we read, "The steps of a good man are ordered by the Lord: and he delighteth in his way." In Jeremiah 10:23 we read, "O Lord, I know that the way of man is not in himself: it is not in man that walketh to direct his steps." In John 14:6 we read, "Jesus saith unto him, I am the way, the truth, and the life: no man cometh unto the Father, but by me." In Romans 9:11 we read, "For the children being not yet born, neither having done any good or evil, that the purpose of God according to election might stand, not of works, but of him that calleth." In Ephesians 2:8–9 we read, "For by grace are ye saved through faith; and that not of yourselves: it is the gift of God: not of works, lest any man should boast." And in John 5:39–40 we read, "Search the scriptures; for in them ye think ye have eternal life: and they are they which testify of me. And ye will not come to me, that ye might have life."

The Masonic Bible says that there is one God, the father of all men. This means the Fatherhood of God and the brotherhood of man. This may sound nice, *but it is blasphemy.*

God is the Creator of all men, but He is the Father only of all those who are saved. God calls some people wicked and some righteous. He calls the saved righteous and the unsaved wicked. He says the saved are with God and the lost are without God. In Ephesians 2:12–13 we read, "That at that time ye were without Christ, being aliens from the commonwealth of Israel, and strangers from the covenants of promise, having no hope, and without God in the world; but now in Christ Jesus ye who sometimes were far off are made nigh by the *blood of Christ.*"

If the fatherhood of God and the brotherhood of man are true, then we are His by virtue of our physical birth. But the Lord shows us in John 3:3, "Verily, verily, I say unto thee, *Except a man be born again, he cannot see the kingdom of God.*"

The Lord describes *the lost man as spiritually blind.* In II Corinthians 4:3–4 we read, "But if our gospel be hid, it is hid to them that are lost; in whom the god of this world hath blinded the minds of them which believe not, lest the light of the glorious gospel of Christ, who is the image of God, should shine unto them."

The lost man is without strength. Romans 5:6 states, "For when we were yet without strength, in due time Christ died for the ungodly."

The lost man is deaf. In Acts 7:57 we read, "Then they cried out with a loud voice, and stopped their ears, and ran upon him with one accord." Jeremiah 6:10 states, "To whom shall I speak, and give warning, that they may hear? behold, their ear is uncircumcised, and they cannot hearken: behold, the word of the Lord is unto them a reproach; they have no delight in it." And in Ezekiel 12:2 we read, "Son of man, thou dwellest in the midst of a rebellious house, which have eyes to see, and see not; they have ears to hear, and hear not: for they are a rebellious house."

The lost man is without hope. We read in Romans 3:23, "For all have sinned, and come short of the glory of God."

The lost man is spiritually dead. Ephesians 2:1 reads, "And you hath he quickened, who were dead in trespasses and sins."

The more you study the Masonic Lodge, the more you must be amazed at the total bankruptcy of it. My biggest surprise in my latest study of the Masonic Lodge is how many churches and groups have taken a stand against them.

I am indebted to Dr. Holly for his books on the lodge and the Southern Baptist Convention. In volumes I and II, I was truly amazed at the length of this list of all the churches who now reject the Masonic Lodge. The Roman Catholic Church is opposed to the Masonic Lodge, but they have their own lodge called "The Knights of Columbus." The following are quotes from pages 21–28:

Lutheran Church—Missouri Synod—In July 1980, the Lutheran Church—Missouri Synod adapted Dr. Philip Lochaas' work on Freemasonry and restated its already-published, strong opposition to the Masonic Lodge. In this report, the Synod listed the Masonic Lodge as "objectionable."

Wisconsin Evangelical Lutheran Synod—In a pastoral theology textbook, *The Shepherd Under Christ*, chapter fourteen is entitled, "The Shepherd and Organizations." In this chapter, Masonic

Lodge membership is rejected because of its "false prayers" and "ungodly fellowship."

Church of the Nazarene—In its *Manual*, revised in 1989, the Church of the Nazarene states: "Membership in oath-bound secret orders or societies: The quasi-religious nature of such organizations dilutes the Christian's commitment, and their secrecy contravenes the Christian's open witness."

The Orthodox Presbyterian Church—In its official publication *Christ or the Lodge?* the committee on Christian Education of the Orthodox Presbyterian Church states, "The committee finds that the evidence presented concerning the religion of Masonry permits but one conclusion . . . that Masonry is a religious institution and as such is definitely anti-Christian . . . membership in the Masonic fraternity is inconsistent with Christianity."

Reformed Presbyterian Church—"Which God? A Brief Statement Regarding Freemasonry" is the title of a tract, which states, "Herein is one of the greatest myths of Freemasonry, that is, that ultimately people of all religions worship and serve the same God." Does Freemasonry hold that there is but one Living and True God? Quite the contrary. It teaches exactly the opposite. Therefore, those who are Freemasons, no matter how unwittingly, give assent to the error that there is more than one True God. And this indeed contradicts the ground of the Christian's confession."

General Assembly Presbyterian Church in America—In answer to Overture 29: From Missouri Presbytery, the Ad Interim Committee rendered the following report in 1988: "No one shall be received into membership into a PCA church who is a member of a Masonic organization. Present members of a church in the PCA who are members of a Masonic organization will be given a period of one year to read the report of the Committee to Study Freemasonry, pray, and consider their membership in the Order in light of the clear statement of incompatibility of Freemasonry with biblical Christianity. After said year, they will be allowed to resign membership or become the subject of formal church discipline."

Synod: Christian Reformed Church in America—A number of excellent statements are available from this denomination about their clear stand on the Masonic Lodge. In the Acts of the Synod, 1974, the following statement is made: "The lodge member who desires to become a member of the church must be kindly but firmly shown that membership in the lodge and in the church of Jesus Christ involves a double commitment which our Lord Himself does not tolerate. Those in the church who affiliate with the Lodge must be shown the error of their way, and if they refuse to repent must be placed under the censure of the church."

Evangelical Mennonite Church—In the *Manual of Faith, Practice and Organization*, the Mennonite Church states: "Membership in any organization—such as the Masonic Lodge—which (1) makes unbiblical promises such as claiming eternal salvation apart from faith in Jesus Christ, (2) imposes unbiblical requirements such as protecting and covering the sin of another member, or (3) teaches unbiblical doctrine such as denying the divinity of Christ, makes one ineligible for membership in the Evangelical Mennonite Church."

The Church of Scotland—The Panel on Doctrine issued the following statement in 1965: "In our view total obedience to Christ precludes joining any organization such as the Masonic movement which seems to demand a whole-hearted allegiance to itself, and at the same time refuses to divulge all that is involved in that allegiance prior to joining. . . . The initiate is required to commit himself to Masonry in a way that a Christian only should commit himself to Christ."

The Free Church of Scotland—This denomination declared: ". . . in the minds of the committee, according to their interpretations of Scripture, membership of Freemasonry . . . is inconsistent with a profession of the Christian faith."

The Baptist Union of Scotland—(endorsed by the Baptist Union of Great Britain and Ireland) " . . . the Council considered the matter carefully and originally agreed that the Doctrine and Inter-Church Relations core groups should review available literature and compile a document directing churches to sources of information, where it was felt guidance was needed.

"However, there were those who felt sufficiently strongly about the question to continue to press for firmer action, and at the Council meeting of January 1987 it was agreed to appoint a group to study the relationship between Masonry and Christianity and to publish their findings in the form of a Viewpoint booklet. They do this in the conviction that our people need clear guidance in this area.

" . . . The important question is not whether Freemasonry is itself a religion, but whether the undoubted religious elements in it can be accepted by a committed Christian without the danger of compromising the Christian faith.

"And why should we wish to belong to a movement which demands of him the kind of commitment that he should only give to Jesus Christ his Lord?

"However, the clear conclusion we have reached from our inquiry is that there is an inherent incompatibility between Freemasonry and the Christian faith. Also, that commitment within this movement is inconsistent with a Christian's commitment to Jesus Christ as Lord."

I know that you can be a believer and commit any sin. David committed adultery and murder and after repentance found forgiveness. But there is something so satanic about rejecting Christ and swearing in the Lord's name with a bloody oath. As a man I can understand moral sin such as stealing, murder, and drunkenness. I can't believe that a person who denies Christ can be saved. A truly blood-bought child of God wouldn't deny the Lord, never, never, no, never! Titus 1:16 says, "They profess that they know God; but in works they deny Him, being abominable, and disobedient, and unto every good work reprobate."

THE BATTLE
AGAINST ARMINIANISM

It seems that most believers, because of a lack of good training and because of a lack of well-prepared pastors, fall for almost anything. Like the residents of Athens, they desire to know something new. In Acts 17:21 we read, "For all the Athenians and strangers which were there spent their time in nothing else, but either to tell, or to hear some new thing." In Hebrews 5:12 we read, "For when for the time ye ought to be teachers, ye have need that one teach you again which be the first principles of the oracles of God; and are become such as have need of milk, and not of strong meat." We also read in Ephesians 4:14, "That we henceforth be no more children, tossed to and fro, and carried about with every wind of doctrine, by the sleight of men, and cunning craftiness, whereby they lie in wait to deceive."

ETERNAL SECURITY

My ship was pulling out of Philadelphia to go to Boston, and I asked my pastor how I could locate a good fundamental Baptist church. He told me to go to a rescue mission because every night different churches ministered at the mission. He told me I could choose the one that I felt was the best. So I found the Dover Street Mission and was told they only had evening services, and they recommended the Ruggles Street Baptist Church for a good morning service.

I was in for a real shock; the church was packed. After prayer, hymns, offering, and special music, the pastor finally spoke. Without a Bible, he began to just talk. He talked about twenty minutes and then finally said, "The Bible says," and I was so uptight that I said, *"Amen!"* It was so *loud* that he lost his train of thought, and he walked off and left the pulpit. When I got to the door, he refused to shake my hand and said in a very loud voice so all could hear, "We do not welcome fanatics or heretics into our church. You are not welcome to come again." I didn't go back.

That evening I returned to the Dover Street Mission for the evening service. The service was just the opposite of the morning service at the Ruggles Street Baptist Church. It was a great service in every way. There was great singing and special music and finally a great message on salvation. At the great invitation I was really flying high, since one of the sailors I had brought to the meeting went forward to be saved.

You would think that nothing could possibly ruin my day, but when the pastor continued the invitation my day was shattered. He said, "Now how about all of you who were *once saved and have now lost your salvation? Will you come forward and get saved again?"* *"What did you say?"* I said out loud. He repeated his words. We then had a verbal war for a long time.

The pastor bombarded me with Bible verses that I could not answer. My friend and I had to leave, so I said to him, "Pastor, I can't answer all of your verses, but I know that you are wrong. I'm going back to my ship, and I will return when I get my answers from the Lord." I had two problems—one, I did not have the answers, and two, my Bible study group was also divided, confused, and they desired answers.

I called my pastor and, as usual, he told me his answer for all problems, "Don't worry, just lead souls to Christ."

I went before the Lord and pleaded for some clear passages in His Word. I began to read the Bible; I started at Genesis and ended at Revelation. I had plenty of time since my ship was moored at Pier One. I did not study the Word; I just *read it* for six hours a day. If I found a verse pertaining to this subject, I would write it down. Then I would go back later to those passages and ask myself why this passage interested me. Of course, our gang gave me no rest. If they saw me ten times a day they would ask me, "Jug, are we ready yet and when will we be ready?" I would reply, "In a few more weeks."

Finally I was ready, and they went nuts with amens, praise the Lords, and hallelujahs. Every sailor in the bunkhouse heard it. I had to remind them that this wasn't a lynching. The first reason was to love and help this misinformed pastor. The second reason was to strengthen our entire Bible study group. The meeting with the pastor lasted three hours, and it was a great meeting. We debated back and forth and finally came to a conclusion: "Convince a man against his will and he will be of the same opinion still."

THE RESULTS OF THE STUDY

Jacobus James Arminius (1560–1609)

- He was a Dutch sea merchant.
- In infancy he lost his father.
- A converted priest took him in; the priest died when he was fourteen.
- When he was fifteen, his mother's sister and two brothers were massacred.
- He then found a home with Peter Bertius, pastor at Rotterdam.
- As a young man he studied under Theodore of Beza, the successor of Calvin.
- He was ordained in Amsterdam, 1588, and became pastor there.
- In 1590 he married the daughter of the Amsterdam city magistrate.
- A study of Romans 7–9 caused him to change from Calvinism to a new theological position.

- In 1609, at the age of 49, he died of tuberculosis and left behind a widow and nine children.

Tenets That Are Commonly Held by
Historical and Modern Arminians

- The image of God in man consists of man's dominion over the law of creation.
- Pollution is inherited from Adam, but his guilt is not imputed to any of his descendants.
- Man's depravity as a result of the Fall should not be described as total.
- Man has not lost his facility of self-determination or the ability to incline his will toward good ends.
- The atonement was not absolutely necessary but represents merely one way among many that God shows how to manifest His love without prejudice to His righteousness.
- There is no imputation of Christ's righteousness to the believer.
- The believer is able to obtain in this life a state of conformity to the divine will in which he may be called perfect.
- As long as man lives, he may fall away from grace and lose his salvation altogether.
- Assurance of salvation is not possible in this life except by special personal revelation.

Arminius was at first a Calvinist but soon became disillusioned and started to teach and preach a new system of doctrine. It was called Arminianism. Arminius made the same error that most of us are prone to make. When we react, we must remember that the sin of reaction is the opposite extreme.

CAN I EVER LOSE MY SALVATION?

What does the Bible say?

- John 10:27–30—"My sheep hear my voice, and I know them, and they follow me: and I give unto them eternal life; and they shall never perish, neither shall any man pluck them out of my hand. My Father, which gave them me, is greater than all; and no man is able to pluck them out of my Father's hand. I and my Father are one."

- Philippians 1:6—"Being confident of this very thing, that he which hath begun a good work in you will perform it until the day of Jesus Christ."

- John 5:24—"Verily, verily, I say unto you, He that heareth my word, and believeth on him that sent me, hath everlasting life, and shall not come into condemnation; but is passed from death unto life."

- John 6:37—"All that the Father giveth me shall come to me; and him that cometh to me I will in no wise cast out." Jesus says here that in no wise will He cast out, *and I believe it.*

- John 6:39—"And this is the Father's will which hath sent me, that of all which he hath given me I should lose nothing, but should raise it up again at the last day." Again Jesus says in this passage that it is His Father's will that He should lose nothing, *no not one.*

In John 10:28 the words *never perish* in God's Word mean *never*; you can be assured of that. In John 4:14 we read, "But whosoever drinketh of the water that I shall give him shall never thirst."

- John 6:35—"And Jesus said unto them, I am the bread of life: he that cometh to me shall *never hunger*; and he that believeth on me shall *never thirst.*"

- Romans 8:1—"There is therefore now *no condemnation* to them which are in Christ Jesus, who walk not after the flesh, but after the Spirit."

- Matthew 7:23—"And then will I profess unto them, I *never* knew you." The Lord *didn't* say, "I knew you, but you couldn't hold on, and you slipped out of My hand." He didn't say that He hoped you would make it, but since you died in that lost condition, you are headed for hell. It is just impossible to live a confident Christian life if you have to keep yourself saved. *Only* our heavenly Father can hold us in His hand s*afely until we die or meet Him in the air.* If we can't do anything to earn salvation, what makes us think we can do something to keep it? What a pity the Arminian robs people of the security God gives them in His Word. When Christ died on the cross, He told the world, "It is finished." It took all of Christ to save and keep us.

SOME QUESTIONS YOU SHOULD ASK AN ARMINIAN

- How many sins must you commit before you lose your salvation? (Arminians don't agree.)
- Are there some sins that are worse than others?
- How do you know when you have lost your salvation?
- Do you know any people in the Bible who lost their salvation?
- Do you believe if a believer committed all of the following sins in a very short time, he would surely lose his salvation?
    Lust
    Stealing
    Adultery
    Deceit
    Murder

Arminianism becomes a stumbling block to many believers. David was a man after God's own heart. David tells us that he lost something. What was it? Psalm 51:12 says, "Restore unto me the *joy* of thy salvation." Notice he did not say return to me "thy salvation" because he didn't lose it. He lost the *joy* of his salvation. He lost the joy that comes with salvation and living completely for the Lord.

The second thing we lose when we allow sin to come and stay is *fellowship.* Isaiah 59:1–2 says, "Behold, the Lord's hand is not shortened, that it cannot save; neither his ear heavy, that it cannot hear: but your iniquities have separated between you and your God, and your sins have hid his face from you, that he will not hear." Sin takes away our fellowship with our heavenly Father. A son who makes his earthly father angry doesn't stop being his son but destroys his fellowship with his father.

Many Arminians say Judas Iscariot was an example of someone who lost his salvation. Judas in John 12:4 was chosen by Christ to be an apostle. Note in this verse, "Then saith one of his disciples, Judas Iscariot, Simon's son, which should betray him." In John 6:64 we read, "But there are some of you that believe not. For Jesus knew from the beginning who they were that believed not, and who should betray him." In verse 70 of John 6, "Jesus answered them, Have not I chosen you twelve, and one of you *is* a devil?" *The Lord could not have been any clearer.*

The false charge by the Arminian against eternal security of the believer is that it gives the saved a license to sin. Arminians say that eternal security means no matter how you live, you can't lose your salvation. One pastor said to me, "Jordan, I have a song for you, "Free from the law, oh happy condition, now I can sin and still have remission." How ludicrous!

In Hebrews 12:1–11 we read,

> Wherefore seeing we also are compassed about with so great a cloud of witnesses, let us lay aside every weight, and the sin which doth so easily beset us, and let us run with patience the race that is set before us, looking unto Jesus the author and finisher of our faith; who for the joy that was set before him endured the cross, despising the shame, and is set down at the right hand of the throne of God. For consider him that endured such contradiction of sinners against himself, lest ye be wearied and faint in your minds. Ye have not yet resisted unto blood, striving against sin. And ye have forgotten the exhortation which speaketh unto you as unto children, My son, despise not thou the chastening of the Lord, nor faint when thou art rebuked of him: for whom the Lord loveth he chasteneth, and scourgeth every son whom he receiveth. If ye endure chastening, God dealeth with you as with sons; for what son is he whom the father chasteneth not? But if ye be without chastisement, whereof all are partakers, *then are ye bastards, and not sons.* Furthermore we have had fathers of our flesh which corrected us, and we gave them reverence: shall we not much rather be in subjection unto the Father of spirits, and live? For they verily for a few days chastened us after their own pleasure; but he for our profit, that we might be partakers of his holiness. Now no chastening for the present seemeth to be joyous, but grievous: nevertheless afterward it yieldeth the peaceable fruit of righteousness unto them which are exercised thereby.

I have been saved for almost fifty-six years, and I have never met a truly born-again believer who *practiced sinning because of his belief in eternal security.* I will forever be indebted to Dick and Martha Mitchell for discipling me. They taught me to test and judge everything by the holy Scriptures.

My wife, Marge, and I have five children. They are Deborah, Timothy, Thomas, Diane, and Tedd. They are all blood Jordans. There is nothing in this world that any of them could do that would make them *not a Jordan.*

Deborah and Diane got married and changed their last name, *but they are still Jordans.*

If Tim, Tom, or Tedd committed terrible crimes against God or country, they would still be *my sons.* If because of these crimes, my wife or I wanted to disown or disinherit them, *they would still be Jordans.*

The Arminian fails to see the difference between *relationship* and *fellowship.* We are related to Christ by the new birth. The moment a sinner repents and receives Christ, he is born into God's family. Galatians 3:26 reads, "For ye are all the children of God by *faith in Christ Jesus.*" We find in John 1:12, "But as many as received him, to them gave he power to become the sons of God, even to them that believe on his name." *Relationship is formed by birth, and nothing can break it.*

Fellowship is formed by the consent of two or more individuals. Webster says fellowship is "the community of interest, activity, friendliness, fellowship of ideals, and goals." The key interpretation is that fellowship is voluntary. Amos 3:3 asks, "Can two walk together, except they be agreed?" *Agreement is essential.* So when you put this into biblical context, it simply means that salvation has to be all of God. Titus 3:5 says, "Not by works of righteousness which we have done, but according to his mercy he saved us, by the washing of regeneration, and renewing of the Holy Ghost." In Ephesians 2:8–9, God does it all: "For by grace are ye saved through faith; and that not of yourselves: it is the gift of God; not of works, lest any man should boast." He saves you, and He keeps you saved. You can only believe and receive His free gift of salvation.

Fellowship is you and God walking together, and it demands walking, obeying, confessing, and knowing the Word of God. You cannot truly walk, work, obey, confess, rejoice, witness, be baptized, and join a local church unless you have a growing knowledge of His Word.

Salvation is strong and cannot be broken because it always depends on Him. Fellowship depends on God and you walking and working together. So sin in the believer's life, whether ignored or enjoyed, breaks fellowship with God and must be confessed and forsaken. First John 1:9 says, "If we confess our sins, he is faithful and just to forgive us our sins, and to cleanse us from all unright- eousness." Proverbs 28:13 says, "He that covereth his sins shall not prosper: but whoso confesseth and forsaketh them shall have mercy."

Now if the sinning believer refuses to repent and return to the Lord, then the final proof that he is truly saved is in Hebrews 12:5–6. "And ye have forgotten the exhortation which speaketh unto you as unto children. My son, despise not thou the chastening of the Lord, nor faint when thou art rebuked of him: for whom the Lord loveth he chasteneth, and scourgeth every son whom he receiveth."

The theme of Hebrews is God's correction of His children. Sal- vation does not stop the believer from sinning, but when the sinner gets saved, God gives him all things that he needs to have victory over living in sin. In II Peter 1:3 we read, "According as his divine power hath given unto us all things that pertain unto life and godli- ness, through the knowledge of him that hath called us to glory and virtue." *He has given us the Holy Spirit for power.* Acts 1:8 states, "But ye shall receive power, after that the Holy Ghost is come upon you: and ye shall be witnesses unto me both in Jerusalem, and in all Judaea, and in Samaria, and unto the uttermost part of the earth."

He has given us the Bible for a complete knowledge of His will. First Peter 1:4 says, "To an inheritance incorruptible, and undefiled, and that fadeth not away, reserved in heaven for you."

He has given us a new nature, the divine nature, II Peter 1:4: "Whereby are given unto us exceeding great and precious promises: that by these ye might be partakers of the divine nature, having escaped the corruption that is in the world through lust."

He has given us a local church for fellowship. We have seen what the Lord does for the believer so that he can have victory. First Corinthians 15:57 states, "But thanks be to God, which giveth us the victory through our Lord Jesus Christ." In II Corinthians 2:14 Paul tells us, "Now thanks be unto God, which always causeth us to triumph in Christ, and maketh manifest the savour of his knowledge by us in every place."

Now we want to see what God does to the believer who sins and refuses to use all these gifts to live a victorious life. Proverbs 28:13 says, "He that covereth his sins shall not prosper: but whoso confesseth and forsaketh them shall have mercy." God gives to each of His children an ability to have an unbroken walk with God.

After you get saved, you will sin. When you do, immediately ask for forgiveness. If you live a life in the power of the flesh, you shall die. In Galatians 6:7–8 we read, "Be not deceived; God is not mocked: for whatsoever a man soweth, that shall he also reap. For he that soweth to his flesh shall of the flesh reap corruption; but he that soweth to the Spirit shall of the Spirit reap life everlasting." Also remember that if you are truly saved, you belong to Him, and He will not share His glory with another. You can never lose your salvation, but you can lose your fellowship. Salvation cannot be renewed or restored, but you can lose your fellowship *many times.* Remember, the lost cannot blame God because God has a sufficient supply of salvation. Christ died for all!

It is possible for believers to live a victorious Christian life because we have an all-sufficient God. Fundamentalists have never held to sinless perfection. The reason is elementary; *it cannot be defended from the Bible.* We believe the Bible teaches that salvation does not destroy the old nature; therefore, the believer will sin. The difference between Jordan before salvation and after salvation is that I was *dead,* and now I am *alive.* Ephesians 2:1 says, "And you hath he quickened, who were dead in trespasses and sins." I was *blind*, and now I can *see*. John 9:25 says, "He answered and said, Whether he be a sinner or no, I know not: one thing I know, that, whereas I was blind, now I see." I was *powerless*. Romans 5:6 says, "For when we were yet without strength, in due time Christ died for the ungodly." I am *powerful*. Acts 1:8 says, "But ye shall receive power, after that the Holy Ghost is come upon you: and ye shall be witnesses unto me both in Jerusalem, and in all Judaea, and in Samaria, and unto the uttermost part of the earth."

TWO SCENARIOS FOR THE BELIEVER

The believer sins and confesses.

- The believer is immediately convicted by the Holy Spirit, as the crowd found in John 8:9, when the Lord wrote in the ground. "And they which heard it, being convicted by their own conscience, went out one by one."
- He chooses to repent and depart from his sin. Proverbs 28:13 says, "He that covereth his sins shall not prosper: but whoso confesseth and forsaketh them shall have mercy."
- He has lost nothing, and he continues his walk with the Lord. Galatians 5:25 says, "If we live in the Spirit, let us also walk in the Spirit." First John 1:7 says, "But if we walk in the light, as he is in the light, we have fellowship one with another, and the blood of Jesus Christ his Son cleanseth us from all sin."

The believer sins against the Lord and does not repent.

- He is immediately convicted by the Holy Spirit.
- He immediately consults the flesh, not the Holy Spirit.
- He believes his sin is not that bad. (Adam and Eve ate only a piece of fruit and died.)

The sinner says, "My sin is not that bad." Galatians 5:19–21 says, "Now the works of the flesh are manifest, which are these; Adultery, fornication, uncleanness, lasciviousness, idolatry, witchcraft, hatred, variance, emulations, wrath, strife, seditions, heresies, envyings, murders, drunkenness, revellings, and such like: of the which I tell you before, as I have also told you in time past, that they which do such things shall not inherit the kingdom of God." Notice that so-called little sins and big sins are bundled together. They are all the same.

God has not judged me for it, so the Lord doesn't care. Look at Ecclesiastes 8:11: "Because sentence against an evil work is not executed speedily, therefore the heart of the sons of men is fully set in them to do evil." Samson thought the same thing, and it killed him.

I can disguise it. The Lord says no in Psalm 139:11–12. "If I say, Surely the darkness shall cover me; even the night shall be light about me. Yea, the darkness hideth not from thee; but the night shineth as the day; the darkness and the light are both alike to thee."

GOD'S REACTION TO THE SINNING BELIEVER WHO REPENTS

Repentance is a change of mind that brings about a change in conduct. A repentant believer always blames himself for sin. In Psalm 51 David uses *me, I,* and *mine* thirty-three times. He did not blame Bathsheba.

A truly repentant person gives a true name to his sin.

- Verse 1—Transgression
- Verse 2—Iniquity
- Verse 2—Sin

Repentance is unconditional and complete. Repenting halfway is not repentance. Being halfway honest is dishonesty. We can't go halfway blaming someone else for our sin. Psalm 51:2 says, "Wash me throughly from mine iniquity, and cleanse me from my sin." The second half of verse 6 says, "Thou shalt make me to know wisdom." Verse 7 says, "Purge me." Repentance will bring about a revived service to the Lord. In verse 13 we read, "Then will I teach transgressors thy ways; and sinners shall be converted unto thee."

GOD'S REACTION TO THE SINNING BELIEVER WHO REFUSES TO REPENT IS TWOFOLD

1. The first reaction is instant conviction.

There is instant conviction by the Holy Spirit. Acts 2:37 says, "Now when they heard this, they were pricked in their heart, and said unto Peter and to the rest of the apostles, Men and brethren, what shall we do?"

You are His child and He will not share you with anyone else or anything. Isaiah 42:8 says, "I am the Lord: that is my name: and my glory will I not give to another, neither my praise to graven images." Psalm 103:8–9 says, "The Lord is merciful and gracious, slow to anger, and plenteous in mercy. He will not always chide: neither will he keep his anger for ever."

2.   The second reaction is that chastisement will follow.

If conviction does not turn the wayward believer around, God will execute chastisement in his life. Hebrews 12:6 says, "For whom the Lord loveth he chasteneth, and scourgeth every son whom he receiveth."

Scourging comes into the sinning believer's life, and he begins to lose. The first thing he loses is his *joy*. Psalm 51:12 says, "Restore unto me the joy of thy salvation." He also loses *power with God*, especially in his prayer life. Samson is an example of this. Psalm 66:18 says, "If I regard iniquity in my heart, the Lord will not hear me." Isaiah 59:1–2 says, "Behold, the Lord's hand is not shortened, that it cannot save; neither his ear heavy, that it cannot hear: but your iniquities have separated between you and your God, and your sins have hid his face from you, that he will not hear."

He loses his *right to the promises of God*. Our Lord said in Matthew 7:7, "Ask, and it shall be given you; seek, and ye shall find; knock, and it shall be opened unto you." Because of sin the Lord cannot give this promise until a person has confessed and forsaken sin. Our Lord said in Jeremiah 33:3, "Call unto me, and I will answer thee, and shew thee great and mighty things, which thou knowest not." The sinning Christian cannot apply Philippians 4:19 to himself because of his sin: "But my God shall supply all your need according to his riches in glory by Christ Jesus."

Why does God chastise the unrepentant believer? Hebrews 12:9 says, "Furthermore we have had fathers of our flesh which corrected us, and we gave them reverence: shall we not much rather be in subjection unto the Father of spirits, and live?" Our heavenly Father chastens us because *He loves us.* And in Hebrews 12:10 we read, "For they verily for a few days chastened us after their own pleasure; but he for our profit, that we might be partakers of his holiness." Our heavenly Father chastises us to produce the fruit of righteousness in our lives. Proverbs 11:30 says, "The fruit of the righteous is a tree of life; and he that winneth souls is wise."

What could happen to the unrepentant believer? He could die! Samson died, Saul died, and Israel as a nation died. Proverbs 1:23–32 says,

> Turn you at my reproof: behold, I will pour out my spirit unto you, I will make known my words unto you. Because I have called, and ye refused; I have stretched out my hand, and no man regarded; but ye have set at nought all my counsel, and would none of my reproof: I also will laugh at your calamity; I will mock when your fear cometh; when your fear cometh as desolation, and your destruction cometh as a whirlwind; when distress and anguish cometh upon you. Then shall they call upon me, but I will not answer; they shall seek me early, but they shall not find me: for that they hated knowledge, and did not choose the fear of the Lord: they would none of my counsel: they despised all my reproof. Therefore shall they eat of the fruit of their own way, and be filled with their own devices. For the turning away of the simple shall slay them, and the prosperity of fools shall destroy them.

We read in II Chronicles 36:15–16, "And the Lord God of their fathers sent to them by his messengers, rising up betimes, and sending; because he had compassion on his people, and on his dwelling place: but they mocked the messengers of God, and despised his words, and misused his prophets, until the wrath of the Lord arose against his people, till there was no remedy."

In the New Testament there is a *sin unto death* when the unrepentant believer refuses chastisement so God exercises His option and takes the *unrepentant believer's life.* First John 5:16 says, "If any man see his brother sin a sin which is not unto death, he shall ask, and he shall give him life for them that sin not unto death. There is a sin unto death: I do not say that he shall pray for it." The sin unto death happens when a believer persists in any sin and is not willing to give it up. Then God takes his life. A good example is found in I Corinthians 11:25–31:

> After the same manner also he took the cup, when he had supped, saying, This cup is the new testament in my blood: this do ye, as oft as ye drink it, in remembrance of me. For as often as ye eat this bread, and drink this cup, ye do shew the Lord's death till he come. Wherefore whosoever shall eat this bread, and drink this cup of the Lord, unworthily, shall be guilty of the body and blood of the Lord. But let a man examine himself, and so let him eat of that bread, and drink of that cup. For he that eateth and drinketh unworthily, eateth and drinketh damnation to himself, not discerning the Lord's body. For this cause many are weak and sickly among you, and many sleep. *For if we would judge ourselves, we should not be judged.*

Walking with the Lord is not easy. When it is done correctly, it is the *greatest life under the heavens*! Christ is the solution to every problem, and I give you Psalm 16:11, "Thou wilt shew me the path of life: in thy presence is fulness of joy; at thy right hand there are pleasures for evermore."

TENETS THAT ARE COMMONLY HELD BY MODERN ARMINIANS

The Image of God

God's divine order is that the believer is to be the image of Christ. Colossians 3:10 says, "And have put on the new man, which is renewed in knowledge after the image of him that created him."

Christ is the visible likeness of the invisible God. Colossians 1:15 says, "[Christ] is the image of the invisible God, the firstborn of every creature." Second Corinthians 4:4 says, "In whom the god of this world hath blinded the minds of them which believe not, lest the light of the glorious gospel of Christ, who is the image of God, should shine unto them." The image of God is true knowledge. In Ephesians 4:24, we see true holiness and righteousness. "And that ye put on the new man, which after God is created in righteousness and true holiness." In John 4:24, we read "God is a Spirit: and they that worship him must worship him in spirit and in truth."

Pollution

Death passed on all. We read in Romans 5:12, "Wherefore, as by one man sin entered into the world, and death by sin; and so death passed upon all men, for that all have sinned." Judgment is found in verse 16 of Romans 5. "And not as it was by one that sinned, so is the gift: for the judgment was by one to condemnation, but the free gift is of many offences unto justification." Romans 5:19 says, "For as by one man's disobedience many were made sinners, so by the obedience of one shall many be made righteous."

Man's Depravity Is Not Complete

Jeremiah 10:23 says, "O Lord, I know that the way of a man is not in himself: it is not in man that walketh to direct his steps." Now if man is almost depraved then maybe he is almost saved. *How ludicrous!* God told us that all men are born dead in sin.

Self Determination

The Arminian is self-determined and will not heed Proverbs 14:12: "There is a way which seemeth right unto a man, but the end thereof are the ways of death."

No Imputation

The definition of *imputation* is "to put down to a person's account, to reckon or to charge good or evil." Romans 4:6, 11, 22–24 says,

> Even as David also describeth the blessedness of the man, unto whom God imputeth righteousness without works. . . . And he received the sign of circumcision, a seal of the righteousness of faith which he had yet being uncircumcised: that he might be the father of all them that believe, though they be not circumcised; that righteousness might be imputed unto them also. . . . And therefore it was imputed to him for righteousness. Now it was not written for his sake alone, that it was imputed to him; but for us also, to whom it shall be imputed, if we believe on him that raised up Jesus our Lord from the dead.

Assurance of salvation is not possible to the Arminian even though Scripture shows us that we have assurance. Philippians 1:6 says, "Being confident of this very thing, that he which hath begun a good work in you will perform it until the day of Jesus Christ." John 6:39–40 says, "And this is the Father's will which hath sent me, that of all which he hath given me I should lose nothing, but should raise it up again at the last day. And this is the will of him that sent me, that every one which seeth the Son, and believeth on him, may have everlasting life: and I will raise him up at the last day."

EPILOGUE

I was somewhat befuddled that as soon as I was saved and the joy of the Lord filled my soul, immediately opposition set in.

Satan tried early in my Christian life to make me doubt my salvation. I had been saved just one day when my division officer came to me and offered me a ten dollar bill. I asked him what it was for. His reply was "Jug, I hear that you got religion last night. Take this ten dollars and go ashore and get drunk. You will soon get over it." I recall being speechless for a second. When I got my voice back, I told him that if I could get over what I got the night before on my knees when I asked the Lord Jesus Christ to forgive me and save me, then I didn't get very much. I gave the money back to him and said, "No, thank you." But from that day on he became critical of me and was unapproachable.

I called my brother and witnessed to him. I thought since he was my brother, he surely would understand. But instead of understanding, he cursed and swore at me and said that he never wanted to see me again. I then called my three sisters and found them to be polite but not interested. They told me I had my life, and they had theirs. It took a while, but praise God, they all received the Lord.

I witnessed to hundreds of sailors aboard my ship, and the vast majority rejected the Lord. The vast majority could be very cruel—

laughing, mocking, and stealing my Bible so I couldn't preach to them. They started false rumors about me, but never to my face, for they knew better. But praise God some believed.

I HAD TO LEARN MANY HARD LESSONS

God didn't save me to win a popularity contest. Luke 6:26 says, "Woe unto you, when all men shall speak well of you! for so did their fathers to the false prophets."

I have no right to expect to be treated better than our Lord. One of the greatest deceptions for the child of God is to believe that he can live the Christian life and at the same time avoid any hurt, persecution, or separation. As soon as a person gets saved, he realizes that he has left one army just to join another. He has left the kingdom of darkness to be a part of the kingdom of light.

LOOKING AT THE WHOLE PICTURE

Before salvation the lost are kept in bondage by Satan. After salvation he knows that he cannot take salvation from believers, so he spends his time and energy standing against any growth in their life. Satan is not omnipresent, omnipotent, or omniscient. He can and should be resisted. Ephesians 6:12 says, "For we wrestle not against flesh and blood, but against principalities, against powers, against the rulers of the darkness of this world, against spiritual wickedness in high places." One of the most serious sins is the failure of the church or the refusal of the soulwinner to teach the new believer a good and thorough Bible course. We seem to be teaching, "Get him saved and then leave him on his own."

Can you imagine a mother praying for a baby, getting pregnant, carrying that child for nine months, going through the travail of delivery, staying in the maternity ward for the acceptable time, *and going home without her child*? We would all wonder why. No decent mother would abandon the baby and say that her job was to have children, *not raise them.* You would say this is impossible and unthinkable, and that would be the right attitude. Yet believers and churches do worse than that. Daily the Lord has commanded the church in Matthew 28:20, "Teaching them to observe all things whatsoever I have commanded you: and, lo, I am with you alway, even unto the end of the world." It seems to me that the church is saying they will lead souls to Christ and let Him make them strong. For this reason, many believers fall into sin and turn back.

When I got saved, I got saved all over—salvation, baptism, church membership—and started serving in a fundamental church and was *trained by four lovely believers.*

I led the music and was taught to teach Sunday school. My soul was saved by Christ, and my life was saved by wonderful believers. How I thank God for the teaching of Dick and Martha Mitchell and Frank and Joy Forrest.

If I was saved right and trained right, I never expected that I would be free from pain, betrayal, sorrow, sin, temptation, and failure. I learned that the believer who was living right could expect the same treatment that the world gave to Christ. I also learned that while the world hated me, the Lord would love me. While the world's promises were shallow and false, all of the promises of Christ were *yea and amen.* While the world's goal was my complete bondage, the Lord's goal was my complete salvation: salvation from the penalty of sin, salvation from the power of sin, salvation from the presence of sin. I was saved about one month when my church began experiencing a real revival. We were having prayer meetings and street meetings, and people were getting saved. Many believers were getting right with the Lord. This made the Devil rear his ugly head. One of our deacons told me that he needed to meet with me. So we met and prayed, and he immediately turned into a tyrant. He wanted to let me know I was ruining the church by all the commotion going on. The church building wasn't built to be used every day. He told me the neighbors were getting upset with all of it, too. *But the last thing he said to me floored me! "Bob, you have the wrong idea of salvation. Salvation is like a match that when you strike it, it flares up, but then it gets down to a slow burn."* I was shocked by his statement. I told him it was OK for us to get excited about baseball, basketball, and football. It was OK to get excited when one of our children got saved. It was OK to get excited about our favorite political party winning a race. *But it was wrong to get excited about being saved and being forgiven, about going to heaven, about having my whole rotten life completely changed, about having a know-so salvation, about being able to pray, and for the first time in my life, knowing He heard me. I told the deacon that if salvation was just a slow burn, I didn't want it. I fully expected my salvation to get "gooder and gooder." Amen! Even my pastor agreed with me.*

CHOOSE TO BATTLE OR LOSE YOUR POWER WITH GOD

These are some of the battles I have fought. When you stop to think of it, every human in the universe is in some battle.

The lost are surrounded by battles, but their only hope is in themselves. Man against himself thinks of getting victory over alcoholism. Watch how he struggles for victory. He swears off a hundred times, only to get captured again. Even Alcoholics Anonymous cannot set him free because when he is free, he must say I am an alcoholic, and I will be an alcoholic. It is a battle until death.

The carnal Christian, the backslider, and the disobedient Christian are in fact saying no to the Holy Spirit. They believe they are OK and can make it through life the way they are.

Think of obesity. No one really knows how many die because they cannot keep their mouths closed. Many have tried just about every diet with little hope. The lost will go through every battle without the Holy Spirit to guide them because they do not read or understand the Bible. They have no Savior to ask for help. It is easy to feel sorry for the lost because they are *blind, deaf, and dead with no hope.*

You feel sorrow for the saved who have heard the Word, believed the Word, obeyed the Word, and then turned away from the Lord. They return to the way of the flesh as Demas did. John 6:66 says, "From that time many of his disciples went back, and walked no more with him." Jeremiah 10:23 says, "O Lord, I know that the way of man is not in himself: it is not in man that walketh to direct his steps."

The conclusion is stated in Ecclesiastes 12:13–14, "Let us hear the conclusion of the whole matter: Fear God, and keep his commandments: for this is the whole duty of man. For God shall bring every work into judgment, with every secret thing, whether it be good, or whether it be evil."

After you get saved, get baptized, join a good, independent, flesh-hating, fundamental Baptist church, put your hand to the plow, and never look back. Lot's wife did and paid a great price. Read your Bible daily. Isaiah 34:16 instructs us to "seek ye out of the book of the Lord, and read." First Thessalonians 5:17 tells us to "pray without ceasing." Learn how. Ask the Lord to let you end your life as Paul did.

I remember hearing our son and pastor, Dr. Timothy Jordan, preach on II Timothy 4:7. I asked his permission to use his literal thoughts of this passage.

A good fight I have been fighting,
my course I have been finishing,
the faith I have been keeping.
AMEN!

RECOMMENDED READING

Battle for the Bible in the 21st Century by R. L. Hymers Jr., published by Hearthstone.

Contending for the Faith by Fred Moritz, published by Bob Jones University Press, Greenville, S.C., 2000.

Stealing Sheep by William Chadwick, published by InterVarsity Press, Downers Grove, Ill.

Cult Watch by John Ankerberg and John Weldon, Harvest House Publishers.

Confronting the Cults by Gordon R. Lewis, published by Presbyterian and Reformed Publishing Co., 1966.

Biblical Separation by Ernest Pickering, published by Regular Baptist Press, 1979.

Can a Saved Person Ever Be Lost? by John R. Rice, published by Sword of the Lord, Murfreesboro, Tenn.

In Christ, but Not Secure? from Homer A. Kent's article in *Spire*, Grace Theological Seminary Winter 1986.

Are Names Ever Blotted from the Book of Life? from Charles Smith's article in *Spire*, Grace Theological Seminary Winter l986.

Once Lost Always Lost? from John A. Sproule's article in *Spire*, Grace Theological Seminary Winter 1986.